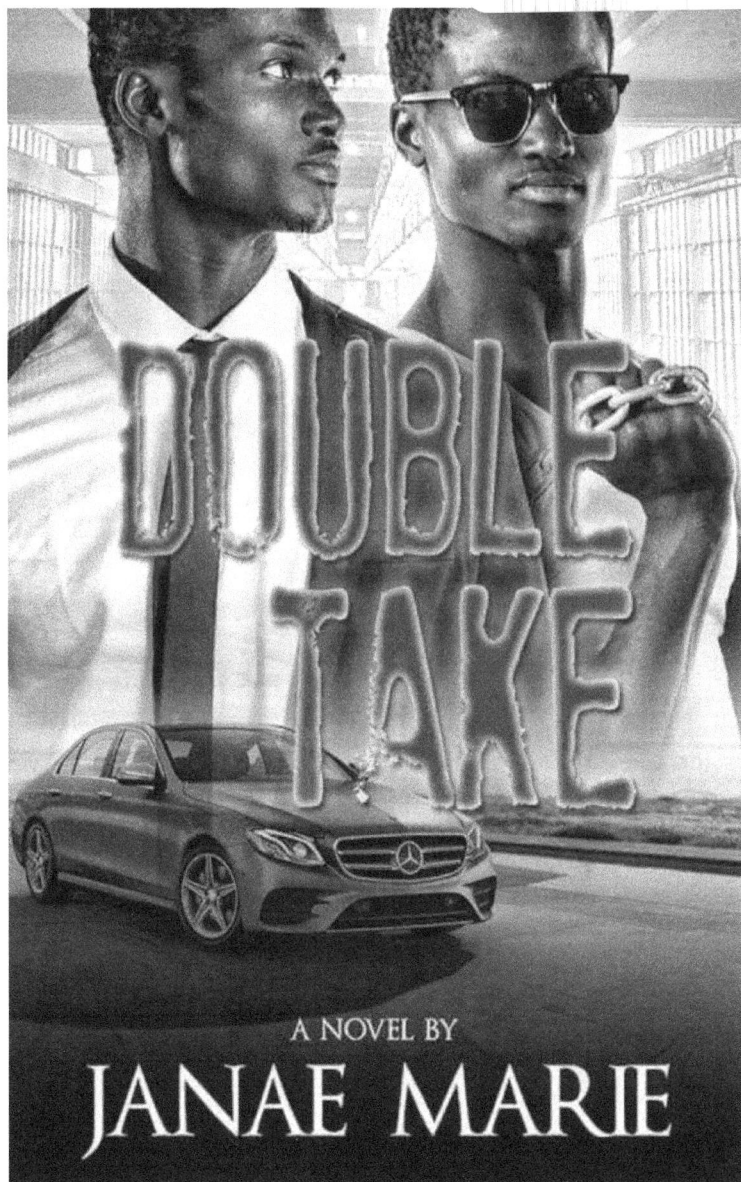

DOUBLE TAKE

A NOVEL BY

JANAE MARIE

This book is dedicated to my wonderful and beautiful little girl, Kayla Hudson.

I hope you are proud.

You can reach Author Janae Marie at
https://janaemariebooks.com

Facebook.com/Authorjanaemarie4519

Twitter: janaemarie5

Instagram: Janae_marie5

CHAPTER 1

TROUBLED MAN

"Dead Man Walking!"

Yeah, I certainly was a dead man walking. I was being sent to jail for about 20 to life for a crime I didn't commit. I was innocent. I swear to God, I was innocent. This was a case of mistaken identity. I've had my share of run-ins with the law, but murder. I'd never do anything that crazy. Well, let me back up and tell you how I get myself into this mess. My name is Karlos Hunter. I'm the twin to my brother and local city councilman Karl Hunter.

It's funny we came from the same home but ended up on two completely different paths. He ended up being a successful politician with a beautiful wife and two kids. Meanwhile, I ended up on the wrong side of the tracks. You'd say I stayed in trouble. I dropped out of high school while my brother went on to graduate with honors from Michigan State University.

But this mess right here, I had no parts of doing, and now I was going to possibly get sent to prison for life. I would be stripped away from my girl Shantae and my baby girl Mariah, who's only five years old. I continued to walk down the corridor as police officers led me to the courtroom to hear the judge's decision. My heart was beating a mile a minute. I couldn't believe this was becoming my life. I saw my lawyer sitting next to me and my girl trying to hold it together while my baby slept on her lap. My lawyer snapped me back into reality as the judge started the case.

"We are here to discuss the case of Karlos G. Hunter vs. The State of Michigan. Mr. Hunter, you're being tried for voluntary manslaughter and if convicted. Hunter, you look to serve up to 20 years to life in prison. Is there anything you'd like to say in your defense?" Judge Abernathy asks me.

"Judge, I didn't kill that girl. I don't even know who this woman is. I was at home with my fiancé and child. I swear…"

"Now Mr. Hunter, this isn't your first time inside my court room. You've had plenty of trouble with the law, and you stand here trying to tell me you didn't do this?"

"Your honor, we honestly don't even have any evidence that Mr. Hunter committed this offense," my lawyer stated.

"Yes, but we do have history. We all know that it was just a matter of time before Mr. Hunter would move on too much bigger crimes," the District Attorney added.

After two weeks of deliberation, the judge convened the trial. Both sides had presented their arguments and the jury had just returned to their seats. The judge addressed the jury by asking, "What is your verdict in the case of the state vs. McKnight?

"We, the jury have found Mr. Hunter...guilty of voluntary manslaughter of Amanda McKnight," a jury foreman said.

I couldn't believe this shit! I was innocent. I didn't even know a damn Amanda McKnight. Now, I had to spend life behind bars for a crime I didn't event commit? What the hell was going on with our damn justice and legal system?

I turned to look at my lawyer. "I told you. I didn't do this."

"I know, I'm going to do everything that I can to see you get victory. They're just going by circumstantial evidence. Don't worry, Mr. Hunter, I'm going to see you get justice," my lawyer promised as two big, burly prison guards started making their way over to me.

"Hey, let me have a word with my brother before you take him away," my brother Karl said.

"Hey Karl, man. I didn't do this, man! I swear to God this is a case of mistaken identity. I told you I wasn't going to let you down no more," I cried.

I promised my brother I'd try to turn my life around and live straight once I became a father.

"You know, Karlos, this really breaks my heart to see you like this. In an orange jumpsuit standing in handcuffs. You really disappointed me. Mom can't even bring herself to come down here to see you like this?"

"But I told you, Karl. I didn't do this. I'm an innocent man!"

"How many times have I heard this line before? What would Shantae think?" he asked me before walking away to join his family. All I could do was stand there crying. My brother just wouldn't believe me. Perhaps, this was my karma for the troubles I've caused the community. Before I was taken away, Shantae, who also had tears in her eyes, came up to me to give me a tight squeeze.

"I didn't do this, baby! I promise, 'Tae. I'm innocent. I'd never kill anybody. I'm not that horrible of a human being."

"I know. I know. I just can't believe they'd pin this on you. They're breaking up my family. What am I supposed to tell Mariah?"

"Just be strong. I promise I'll be out of here soon," I said to her and gave her a kiss on the lips before the guards escorted me out of the courthouse.

I was on my way to prison with my heart trembling in my chest. All I could see was my life flashing before my eyes. Since I've told you so much, let me tell you a little bit about my troubled past.

CHAPTER 2

10 YEARS AGO

Back Down Memory Lane

From what I remember, the moment my life was beginning to go south started with my senior year in high school.

Karl and I were getting ready to start our day. As usual, he was running around the house to go off to Cass Technical High School. But me, I was in my room bumping that West Coast joint. Tupac and Dr. Dre., *California Love.* As I was nodding my head to the music, my mom bust in the room shutting off my damn music!

"Dammit, boy! Cut that rap crap off and get your behind down to that school. I told you that you had to keep your behind in school this year. Hell, you barely made it to the twelfth grade! At this rate, you're either going to be dead or in jail. You better than this, Karlos."

"Ma, I'm not feeling school--" Before I finished my sentence, she slapped me lightly across the face.

"You better do what I tell you, Karl! Come on in here and speak to your brother. I can't believe two twin boys who came from the same mother can act so differently," my mom argued before she walked off frustrated.

My little kiss-ass brother walks into my room and stares directly at me. I knew what he was about to say, and I wasn't trying to hear it. I didn't have time for that corny stuff.

"Man, Karlos what's going on with you? How come you won't get your act together?"

"I'm not trying to hear that mess, man. I'm about that trap life. I gotta get money. Why should I sit in a classroom listening to some old-ass people talk when I could be on the streets hustling? I'm a boss man, I get money."

"Man, you're not making any sense. You could be using your brain to get money. Instead, you're going to get yourself messed up, man." Karl tried to counsel me all of the time. I knew we didn't have a pops, but I didn't need my twin brother trying to "mentor" me all of the time. Sometimes I just wish he'd be my damn brother instead of this little goody-two shoes.

"Man, alright Karl, let's go. I rather go to school than listen to you talk about school."

Karl and I made our way down to school, but while he had thoughts of being this great "I AM" somebody, all I could think of was getting money and owning my neighborhood. See, I had no worry for education; that white-washed fabricated man-made education. I was going to find ways to get mine, even if it meant hustling on the block.

As we approached Cass Avenue, I ran into a few partners I hung out with from time to time. These were the kingpins, hustlers and dope boys, everything my brother hated and tried to get me to stay away from. But they lived a life I could see myself becoming accustomed to. They had the women, money and cars. I deserved that lifestyle, and I was going to get it through any means necessary.

"Hey what's up, Karlos? Why don't you come on over here and let me holler at you real quick? I might got some work for you," my boy Quincy yelled out to me. But before I could even reply Karl shouts back…

"Naw, man he can't go with you. He got school."

I looked over to him in disbelief. "Q, I'll catch up with you, man."

"Oh' alright, Karlos, man. I got you." Karl shoves me into the direction of the school. We walk down the hallway after being checked through the metal detectors.

"Man, you really need to check who you call your friends. Trust me, bro, that dude ain't your friend. He going to have you caught up in these streets. I'm trying to tell you."

"Man, I'm 17 years old. I'm a grown-ass man. I don't need you trying to tell me how to run my life. Let me do me."

"I'm just trying to help," Karl replied.

"Thank you, Daddy," I answered.

"Come on, let's go to class before we're late," Karl warned.

But I had other plans. As I was walking towards the Chemistry class, I laid eyes on the finest woman I had ever seen. She was a little brown-skin cutie with shoulder length hair. She had the darkest and most beautiful brown eyes I'd ever seen. This girl's body was completely on-point from head to toe. I had to holler at her.

I could see my brother getting annoyed, but I just told him I'd catch up with him later. While he walked off into class, I slowly approached this sista' hoping to get a name to such a fine-ass face.

"Excuse me, miss lady, I don't think I've seen you here before. What's your name?" I questioned, hoping to win her over.

"What really? I heard all about you, Karlos Hunter," she retorted, walking away.

"Hey, how do you know me? What'd you hear about me?"

"You know, just stuff." She smiled and began walking towards her locker. She messed with her combination lock. I stood right beside her. I was going to make this girl mine even if it took me all semester to do it.

"Well, what they tell you about me, sweetheart?"

"Oh, I see you not the type that gives up, huh?" She smiled again. She had such a beautiful smile.

"That you were, um…that you get around."

"Huh, that's all a lie. I don't have time for that. I try to stay on top of my money. I chase paper. Not women. NO offense. But those are rumors. Don't listen to rumors. So, can I call you some time?" I joked, but seriously hoping she'd give the digits. She rolled her eyes then pulled out her cell phone.

We exchanged numbers, and I even got a hug from her before she made her way to French class.

"You want me to carry your books for you?"

"It's ok. My class is just the next two doors down. But thank you anyway."

"Hey, you didn't tell me your name?"

"Shantae Harris!"

"I'll call you later, Shantae." I smiled like a kid in a candy store. I had to make Shantae mine. She was smart, sexy and mature. Everything I needed in a girl. But while I was day dreaming about Shantae, my boys Allen and Teri brought me back to reality.

"Man, what are you doing? Stop thinking about pussy when it's paper to be made around here. I told you my boy Quincy would put you on," Allen tried to persuade me to join him in the drug game. As much as I wanted the money, I tried to avoid it. But the amount of cash they make on a regular, sometimes brought me back to where I needed.

"So, are you in or what? My man looking for a few more people. And I know how you love getting money, man. You could be rolling in a brand-new Impala, clocking in those thousands of dollars, man. The money don't sleep. All you gotta do is move a few units. You in there?" Teri also added.

As usual, I told them that this was something that I had to think about. I really was trying to stay out of my mom's hair until I got out school. But there were some things that began to change my mind.

Later That Day

Back at Home

After we ate dinner, my brother and I were in the kitchen washing dishes when we heard our mother crying. Karl and I stopped to see what was making our mother, a woman who's as strong as a mule, cry.

"Naw, Mom, what's the problem?" Karl asked.

"I just can't do it anymore. I'm working, but it's just not enough money for me to keep things going," she cried.

"Mom, what are you talking about?" I questioned, concerned.

She sadly pointed to an envelope that read in big, bold red letters: PAST DUE...FINAL NOTICE.

"They're threatening to cut off the lights if we don't pay the $364, and if we don't come up with the rent by next week, we're going to get evicted."

"Mom, why didn't you tell us things were this bad?" Karl spoke out.

"Because it's my job to keep it together for you two boys. I just didn't want you to worry. Plus, it's not your responsibility. I was trying to pull in more hours at work, but it just wasn't enough. Now, I don't know what to do.

Listening to my mother stress over shit like bills and rent made me decide what to do with my

life real quick. I had to be a man. I had to help out.
A man does what a man has to do. Right now, this
man had to come up with some cash…quick. At
that moment I knew exactly what I had to do to get
it.

CHAPTER 3

A MEETING WITH QUINCY

I walked out of my mother's room and headed to my room. I was devastated that my mom was going through something like this. My mom was the strong type, so for her to come breaking down like this must've meant she really needed help.

Karl walked in to see how I was doing.

"Hey man, are you alright?"

"Look, I don't know about you, but I gotta do what I gotta do as a man to bring some money in around here."

"Hey, I know you're frustrated, Karlos, but we're doing the best we can. I have a job myself—
"

"What you talking about? That little McDonald's job you got down at the mall? Man, that $8 an hour bullshit ain't going to get you nowhere. We need REAL money," I yelled at him.

"Well, what the hell do you suppose we do?" he questioned, walking over to me. I could tell I was beginning to strike a nerve with my brother. But I didn't care, I wanted to make shit happen. I got tired of struggling everyday while others got to live comfortably. Naw man, fuck that. It was time for a change.

"I know how to make some shit happen. I got a way to bring some cash up in here."

"I know you aren't talking about selling no drugs! If that's your way of making REAL money, you can just forget it, Karlos. We just need to get jobs and—"

"Jobs? Fuck a job! I'm not busting my ass for no damn minimum wage pay that still won't be enough. Naw, bruh, I'm going to do things my way."

"And what? Get shot or end up dead because that's all that's going to happen. Be smart. I'm going to go to college, major in political science. I'll become a politician and truly change shit around here. Not contribute to the crime that's already going on in the world," my brother rattled off.

I could feel the anger raging in my chest. I try not to explode sometimes, but I just couldn't stand how blind my brother was. I tried to get him to see shit the way I did, but his perception of the real world was so skewed.

"You know, you always try to act like you're so damn perfect. Like you're so damn better than me. But let me tell you the truth, the reality of shit around here. We two black brothers from the streets of Detroit. Ain't nobody taking us seriously. We ain't changing shit. No doors opening for us. We got to do what we can to survive out here, son," I hopefully enlightened my very naïve brother.

"Well, you think what you want to think. I just know you get a lot further in life by using your brain than trying to hustle on the streets. But you do your thing and see which one of us lasts longer out here," he replied back before walking out like a little bitch. He was always so "conscious."

People called us Huey and Riley, and I'm sure by now you can understand why. I was a hellraiser who didn't take shit from anyone. I've been in more fights than anyone I knew. I've been expelled from three different schools. My brother, on the other hand, was a little kiss-ass in my opinion. Always doing good, studying and staying on the honor roll. He even got a full-ride scholarship to the college of his choice. Me, I didn't care about pursuing no education. Don't no black man got business being inside a white man's educational prison system.

Later the Next Day

While everyone was gone and I was supposed to be in school, I had other plans. I wasn't going to let the lights get cut off or we get evicted. So, I made a call to a friend.

"Yo, Al, your boy still looking for people to work for him?"

"Cool, cool. I'll be there in fifteen minutes," I said, ending my call.

I grabbed my keys and wallet and was out the door. As I made my way down to meet Allen, who drove me to Fenkell & Wyoming to meet up with his boy Quincy, I began to feel nervous about what I was about to do. But then images of my mother weeping in pain brought me back to reality. I was doing this for us and no one else.

"You good, my man?" my boy, Allen, asked me as he pulled up to the curb in a brand-new Audi 216.

"Wait, whose car is this?" I questioned.

"Duh, who else? Mine, my brother."

I hopped into the car and we took off down the street. But I couldn't help but wonder how my boy, who is only 18 years old his damn self, was able to afford such an expensive-ass car.

"I know, but how. You ain't got no—"

"Come on, Karlos man, when you're good, money is good. Plus, Quincy hooks up his people real nice. That's why you need to come work for us. Forget that job shit. You're not going to make the amount of money you deserve to get," he persuaded with a sly grin upon his face.

I took in what he had to say. We did need the money. We finally pulled up to this nice duplex house on the corner of Fenkell.

"When we get in there, it'll be Quincy and a few of his business men. Don't be scared. If he thinks you too scared, he won't want to work with you. So be confident. Show some heart. You know, be a man," Allen warned me. As we approached the front door, we were greeted by a fair-skinned, stocky guy with a medium build, about 5"10. I could tell he ate...a lot. But he appeared to be the gatekeeper between me and Quincy.

"Hey Allen, who is this dude? You know Q is funny about everybody that come through here."

"Naw, it's good. This here my boy, Karlos. Remember I told you about him," Allen said to reassure this burly guy that my presence was safe.

"Ooh yeah, okay. Come right on in, Karlos. Quincy been waiting to see you," he told me.

"Alright thanks, Juan...It's through here. That's where Q is." Allen pointed to a door to the right down the hall. We walked in and saw Quincy, a tall, slender and clean-cut brother counting money on this electronic device I had never seen before in an office. I assumed this was where he counted his money and checked his henchmen.

"Close the door behind you," he called out to us.

"Anytime I'm counting my money, the door stays shut. I don't even take visits during this time, but your boy Allen over here told me that you needed some cash. And I thought to myself, why not me? There's no one better than myself to offer a helping hand to this brother. Plus, I've been trying to recruit you for the longest," he laughed and looked up at me.

"Hey Allen, why don't you let me talk to your boy Karlos here alone."

After Allen shut the door behind him, he ordered me to sit down in a chair beside him.

"Now look, I heard all about your problems trying to pay the rent. I know your brother Karl trying to keep you away from me. He wants to steer you on the right path. But who said his path was necessarily the best path to take?" he stated as he began to light a cigar.

"I'm not trying to tell you to turn on your brother or nuthin like that. But it's real out here in these streets. We black men got to survive the best way we know how. I'm trying to get out the game myself. Man like me getting too old to keep running these streets. I got me a girl. I'm trying to retire and move to Brazil or some shit, ya feel me?

He laughed hard while taking a long pull of his cigar.

"All I'm saying is, with a little bit of coaching from me, I can have you king of these here streets. You'll be the most respected and feared dude out here. I know you got that little fight up in ya. Just so you know, I'm not playing. Here's a little gift from me to you, just to get you started."

Quincy handed me an envelope of $600 cold, hard cash. I couldn't believe it. I had never made this much in a day. This would certainly be enough to pay our light bill now.

"I know that this ain't much, but just think what more you can get working for me? You saw what your boy Allen riding in. I take good care of my employees. I need you here at 9 a.m. to pick up your product. I collect at the end of the week. I expect more than $500.00 every week. You understand me?" he asked me sternly, staring into my eyes. I could tell Quincy was serious when it came to his cash.

"Don't play with my money. I'm a nice guy. You want to keep it that way, you hear me?"

"Yeah, yeah. I hear you Quincy. I got you," I assured him.

"Good. I'm glad to see we're on the same page."

Quincy gave me some dap and I exited out of the room. If this was all I had to do to get my hands-on Benjamins, I could have started doing this shit months ago. Little did I know the troubling problems that awaited in my future just because of my involvement with this.

CHAPTER 4

A LOVE BLOSSOMS

A few months had passed, and I was doing well. I kept money between me and Karl, and my mother never had to worry about another bill. I was able to provide for the household and keep a little something for myself. I even began a relationship with my girl, Shantae. So, yea, everything was going well…

At the dinner table, I surprised my mom with a 24k carat gold necklace that read, "I love you, Mom" plus a little cash, around $250 stuffed inside an envelope. The look on her face was worth every penny. But of course, my brother had to butt in with his hating ass.

"Where you getting all this money from for all these 'gifts' Karlos? Last time I checked you didn't have a job. So, where this money coming from, man?"

"That's right, Karlos, this ain't no drug money, is it? You know I don't want no parts of dirty money up in my house. This is a Christian house. Don't be bringing those devil spirits in here," my mother exclaimed.

"Of course not, Mom, I wasn't going to tell anyone because I was a little embarrassed but since Karl brought it up, I did get a job. I got a job working at KFC a couple weeks ago, and I've been just saving to buy some gifts. Just to show you my appreciation," I lied.

There was no way I was going to ever tell my mother the truth.

"Oh, that's nothing to be ashamed of. I'm so proud of you. Thank you, Karlos!"

"Well, since we're all in such good spirits, I thought I, too, would share my good news. My acceptance letter came in the mail today. I'm going to be a freshman at Michigan State University, with a Political Science major," my brother rambled out. Always had to brag. Always gotta upstage me on some shit as much as I had love for his ass. Sometimes I couldn't stand his punk ass.

"Oh, this is wonderful! I can't believe my son Karlton Hunter is going to be a freshman in college. This is just amazing. I gotta go call everybody with the good news," my mother shouted as she left the table to go phone her sister and all her friends.

I just sat across the table fuming at my brother, ready to punch his lights out.

"You always gotta steal my shine, don't you?"

"Well, it's not like it's hard to do. And where do you get off lying to Mom like that? You might can fool her, but you can't fool me. Man, I know you don't work for no damn KFC or no other damn place. So, tell me where the hell are you getting this damn money from?"

"None of your damn business!" I yelled at him as I left to go to my room.

"Don't tell me you're selling drugs? You must not want to live to see 21, Karlos! You always gotta be the bad seed. Why must you always be the fuck-up in our family?" Karl mouthed off a little too damn much for me tonight. Fueling fire to the flames, I turned around and socked him in the jaw. We started fist fighting.

"You always got to be a little goody two-shoes. You act like a little bitch."

"Don't get mad at me because I'm excelling at life and you ain't going to become shit with yourself."

"Fuck you!"

We began fighting some more before our mother came in to break us up.

"What the hell is going on in here?"

"He started it?" Karlton blurted out.

"Naw, no I didn't," I replied back in defense."

"You know, I don't care who started it. Your brothers and you shouldn't be fighting, now apologize," she ordered.

I just sat there on my bed breathing hard, staring at Karlton. Praying for a round two.

"Dammit, I said apologize! Don't make me get my belt!"

"Sorry," my punk-ass brother shouted out.

"Karlos apologize to your brother!"

"Sorry!"

"That's better, now you two knock it off and go to bed. It's late," our mother said before she and Karlton left my room.

Even though I was still upset with Karlton, the one person I knew would put a smile back on my face was my girl Shantae. I called her up hoping she'd be home. She picked up on the third ring.

"Hello!"

"Hey baby, I see you miss me. You picked up quick," I teased her.

"Shu up, what are you doing?!"

"Nothing, just lying down. I just got into a fight with Karlton, my twin brother."

"Oh no, what were you guys fighting about?"

"Same old bullshit. Don't worry about it. When am I going to get a chance to see you again?" I smiled. I could feel this girl was special. She turned my whole day around just with the sound of her voice.

"Well, how about tomorrow? My parents will be at work all day and my sister is out of town. So, that's perfect timing for us."

"It sure is, damn. I can't wait. You got me thinking about it already. I really miss you."

"I miss you, too, Karlos."

"Well, I know I'll be dreaming about you tonight, most definitely. I'll see you tomorrow," I said ending our conversation.

The Next Day

I headed over to see Shantae over in the Oak Park area in Detroit. She had a good future. Why she wanted to be with a guy like me? Who knows? But all I know was, she brought out the best in me. We met up at the Dairy Queen place to grab some ice cream, then walked down the street to her house. I might have only been 17, but I knew what I wanted. At this moment, I wanted Shantae.

We sat on the couch finishing up our ice cream and just talking.

"You ever been with a guy like me before?" I questioned staring into her eyes.

"What do you mean like you? What about you?"

"You know, I'm sure you've heard all about me. I'm a bad boy. I stay in trouble all the time. You're such a good girl, why you bothering yourself with someone like me?

"Because I like you, silly. I don't see what you see about yourself. You see a bad guy. I see someone with a troubled past but with so much potential to be and do more in life. I think you're a good person," she explained to me. At that moment, I knew that she was the girl for me. She always lifted me up whenever I felt down. I'd be a damn fool to let that slip away. Naw, I had to be sure to lock her down. I leaned to kiss her soft lips while she ran her hand down my back.

I whispered in her ear that we should go upstairs. I made sure to lock the door behind us. I grabbed Shantae by the waist and pulled her close to me. We began kissing passionately. I slowly rubbed my hands all over her body. I wanted her right now. She threw me on the bed and began to undress for me. I started to feel my dick getting hard as shit. The more she came on to me, the hornier I could feel myself get. She climbed on top of me then proceeded to take my clothes off. I kissed her softly on the neck until I reached her breasts. When she ran her hand down my chest, I motioned for her to get positioned on the bed. She placed my dick inside of her tight, wet pussy and started riding me like a horse. This shit felt good. I couldn't believe how skilled she was. Shantae planted gentle kisses on my neck and behind my ear and glided her tongue down my chest.

I could feel myself growing harder by each vibration of her movement. I lay her down on the bed and got to work. Once back inside, I started giving it to her. The moans she cried and my name she screamed made this moment even more pleasurable. She quietly told me she loved me as she whispered excitedly in my ear. As good as I was feeling right now, hell, I returned the compliment. While I stroked inside of her, I kissed all over her body and I was getting it in good.

I picked her up, wrapped her legs around my waist and started fucking her up and down in the air. The farther I stroked, the tighter she held on to me. When I couldn't hold her anymore, I placed her body on the floor and made love to her until she told me that she was ready to cum, which only made me drive harder to help her reach that climax.

As I caressed my fingers against her clitoris, the louder she screamed and the faster I felt myself about to nut. She grabbed me tighter and we came together. We laid out on the bedroom floor, and all I could think of was that amazing-ass sex we just had. I planted a kiss on her forehead and she laid on top of me as we both fell asleep together.

CHAPTER 5

FRIEND OR FOE

I was beginning to enjoy this life I'd created for myself since I started working for Quincy. Everything became easier. Things began to multiply in my eyes. I became popular. Everybody knew me. I was the man around these streets. I could've taken Q's place. I had more money than a normal kid like me should have, and I was enjoying every minute of it.

Finishing up my last round, I decided to head back to Q's place, but he found me first. He was in the backseat of an all-black Audi 216 and motioned for me to get inside the car and talk with him.

"So, how you doing this afternoon? You got all my money?" he questioned me stiffly.

"Yeah, Quincy. I got it all right here." I handed him a wad of money.

"Always loyal. I like that. I don't have to worry about you stealing shit from me. I admire that from the dudes that work for me. I reward that. You know, I heard you got a little lady around here. You definitely got to have a car, be able to pick her up and take her out." He smiled while he handed me the keys to a brand new red Chrysler 300c.

I didn't know what to think, I never owned a car before. And after he told me everything was paid and taken care of by him, I couldn't do anything but drop a few tears. I got out the car to see my car parked alongside the curb. This was the best present I'd ever received from anyone. I really looked up to Quincy. He was somewhat like a father figure. He had a plan for his life, and he was out making shit happen for himself through any mean necessary.

Later that day, I drove my car home and was all smiles for the rest of the evening. I was in such a good mood that not even my hating ass brother Karlton could steal my joy.

"Hey," my brother says.

Speak of the devil, my brother knocks on the door and peeks his head in while I'm playing a game on Xbox.

"What do you want? I'm busy," I replied with an attitude.

"Yeah, I see that." He rolled his eyes at me.

"Um, you wouldn't happen to know whose car that is parked in front of the house would you."

"Yeah, it's mine."

"What do you mean, "It's mine?" You can't even afford a car…or drive a car that expensive!"

"Why not? We were both licensed a year ago. What are you talking about? Besides it was a gift."

"A gift, gift from who? I hope you're not talking about that Quincy dude I've been seeing you with lately. That dude is bad news. I hope you're not hanging out with him. I'm just trying to protect your future."

"Look, I'm damn near grown. I don't need my twin brother looking out for me. I'm not twelve." I shouted back.

"I know how fucking old you are. We were born on the same day. I just care about you. Why you got to be so selfish all the damn time? All you think about is yourself, Karlos!"

"Yup, and money and Shantae. What, you jealous that I'm making more money doing what I'm doing than you working your little whack McDonald's job? Here, you need some cash? Take some and get the hell out my face," I yelled back throwing a wad of twenty-dollar bills at my brother.

"You know, you may think you're doing good now, but all this fast money isn't good money. One day, all this is going to catch up with you, and when you get caught up, best believe your 'boy' Quincy won't be there to save your dumbass. You better learn how to listen and stop being so damn hard-headed," he warned me.

Somehow, at the back of my head, I knew he was right but being young, dumb and stubborn, I just didn't want to listen to my brother. Little did I know, that thing called karma would soon come biting me in the ass.

The Next Week

I was on the block doing my thing like I always did. Nothing seemed out of the ordinary to me. I was on the corner of Dexter near Linwood when a black car pulls up asking for a dime bag. I pull my regular routine, but something went wrong because the next thing I knew the dudes come out flashing a "DPD" badge. Damn, I fell for the okey-doke. I was getting arrested and thrown in the back seat of a squad car.

I couldn't believe this shit was happening to me right now. After I arrived at the precinct, I was taken to this room. They took the cuffs off me and told me to sit my black ass down. The arresting officer sat across the table from me interrogating me.

"So, tell me kid, what's your name?"

All I knew I wasn't giving up any information. No snitching around my hood.

"They call me G. Hunter," I lied to play tough, but deep down I was scared shitless.

"Oh really, G. Hunter, according to the file we just checked, your name is Karlos."

"Well, if you knew that already, why'd you ask me? That's pretty dumb," I retorted with a grin on my face.

"Oh, you're trying to be a smart ass, huh?! You know, I was going to let you go with a warning since you don't have a record. But now, just for that remark, I might have to hold you for a couple days. Teach you a lesson. Tell me kid, who you working for out there on those streets?"

He continuously interrogated me.

"I don't know. I don't work for anybody."

"Son, I've never seen you around these streets. I can tell you're new, so, I'm sure you work for someone. The drug lords are never on the street pushing their own shit. I mean, have you ever seen the CEO of McDonald's at a restaurant trying to persuade new customers to try their food. Hell no, and you never will. They hire other motherfuckers for that shit. So, back to the question at hand, who do you work for?"

"I just told you, I work for myself."

"Dammit, son! Look you don't want to end up here trying to catch some damn 'street cred.' Trust me, the low-life dirt bags that you're trying to protect don't give a damn about you and will probably rat your young naïve ass out in a heartbeat to cover their own asses. So, don't be dumb."

I simply rolled my eyes and shrugged my shoulders. The officer, who was an overweight, balding white guy with glasses on and bad breath, got real close to my face and said something that would begin my downward spiral into life.

"If you don't confess, we're going to have to hold you for ninety days."

"Wait, I thought you said just a couple days. Now, I'm going to here for three months? What the hell?!" I screamed out.

"I can't be in here for no damn three months! I got my…I got to make a phone call. I know I get a phone call!"

"If you simply comply with our orders, you could be out of here within a couple days like I said."

I didn't want to go to nobody's jail, but then I thought about how Quincy said he respected loyalty out of me. I couldn't let him down after everything he'd done for me. Hell naw, what's 90 days? It was time I manned up and faced reality.

After an hour or so of ruthless interrogation, the officers realized that I wasn't going to confess to shit, so they allowed me to make my phone call. I explained to Karlton everything that went down. He tried to give me some dumb-ass lecture about following the wrong crowds, but I wasn't trying to hear that shit. They cuffed me back up and walked me to a holding cell, which consisted of a bunk bed and a damn urinal. The officers removed the handcuffs and threw me in the cell and slammed the gate. I was in jail. In jail for ninety fucking days. All I could think about was my mother and my girl Shante.

After a couple of hours of being confined to these dingy, gray prison walls, I didn't know what the hell I was thinking. There was no way in hell I'd survive ninety days in here. Things would get worse before they ever got any better. I sat and contemplated what my mother could possibly be thinking of me right now.

CHAPTER 6

KARL'S STORY

I couldn't believe this mess. My brother had gotten himself thrown in jail. I don't know how many times I've tried to talk to him. He was stubborn as a mule. Thrown in jail over some meaningless bull for trying to protect people who don't even care about him. I walked into the house and looked my mother straight in the eyes and drummed up all the courage I could to tell her this news I had.

"Karlton, where's your brother? I haven't seen or heard from him all day. Usually he at least checks in once a day to let me know he made it down to the school," my mother questioned.

"Mom, um…I have something to tell you." This was hard to say. How do you tell your mother that her son has just become a part of the system?

"Um, I talked to Karlos earlier today…he's in jail."

"JAIL!!!!!" my mother screamed out with a surprised look on her face. I couldn't believe it either.

"Yes. Something about drug possession and not cooperating with the cops. He's going to be in there for about 90 days."

"What?! Drugs! How many times have I told that boy to stay out of trouble? Why doesn't he listen? Now he got a record and…. Let me go and get my baby out of that place."

It broke my heart having to first inform our mother why Karlos had yet to come home. We even went down to the precinct hoping to handle things and even post bail if need be. But because of his actions, he had no choice but to complete his 90-day stint in jail. We later returned home, in disbelief and worry. I tried to sleep that night, but all I could think of was my brother and how they were treating him. I could just imagine what was going through his mind. No matter how tough my brother pretended to be on the outside, he was a soft as a marshmallow on the inside.

Later the next day at school, after I had gotten out of my Physics class, I looked around to find Karlos's girlfriend Shantae. She had called a few times last night wondering why she hadn't heard from him yet. Unfortunately, I had to be the one to tell her she wouldn't be hearing from him for a while. I caught up with her at her locker as she was preparing to go to English class.

"Hey, Shantae, how are you doing?" I questioned nervously.

"Oh hey, Karlton. I'm fine, but I tried to reach your brother last night. He never returned my call. What's going on with him?"

"Um, I have some bad news, Tae."

"What is it?" Her eyes widen as I spoke.

"My brother got himself arrested…something about drug possession and not cooperating with cops. He's going to be in there for at least 90 days. That's why you haven't heard from hi m. We've already tried to go see him and post bail, but they won't let us."

"WOW! I can't believe this. This is so crazy. I tell that boy all the time to stay out of trouble. But he just doesn't listen. Thank you, Karlton. I appreciate you telling me what's going on, really. Just please keep me updated on what's going on with him."

I promised Shantae I would keep her updated on his whereabouts until he gets out.

She was furious at Karlos for putting himself in the situation he was in. I really prayed that my brother would learn his lesson after all of this. But if I know my brother, he'd probably brush it off like it's nothing and go right back to doing the same old thing.

CHAPTER 7

COMING HOME: KARLOS

Three Months Later

Man, this was the dumbest mistake I'd ever made. Being in jail certainly wasn't for me. I couldn't take this solitary confinement, crazy-ass inmates and nasty-ass food. It wasn't shit for me to do in here but think. So, I thought a lot. I'd make sure I'd never end up in here or worse.

Well, ninety days had finally come and gone. I saw the guard opening the gate to bid me my freedom. Who did I see waiting for me? My brother, Karlton. He had a disgusted look on his face, but he showed up to come get me. He kept his word like he said he would. Like a real brother. We walked outside to see a blue Dodge Neon parked across the precinct.

"Whose car is this?" I questioned

"Mom got her sister to lend me the car. We didn't tell her what it was for though. I'm just glad you're out, going home and hopefully learned from this. I hope you won't do anything dumb like this again. You're too young to have a record, but that's what you got now," my brother scolded me like a father as we walked towards the car.

"Man, just drive me home," I replied to get him to shut up.

As we approached the house, I could see my mother's disappointment. It was marked all over her face. I took a seat in the dining room, and all my mother could say was how upset she was with me.

"What the hell would possess you to carry drugs? Are you trying to throw your life away? Now, you know I raised you and you brother better than that. If you plan to stay in this house, you have got to clean up your act, boy, or your next steps will be on the streets or back in jail or worse, dead. I'm so tired of young black men throwing their lives away. Get it together, boy. Get it together please, Karlos," she warned me before leaving to go to her room.

I honestly think a tear fell from my eye listening to how disappointed in me she was. I vowed to myself to never let her feel this way again.

A week later, I went to go see my girl, Shantae. She wasn't too happy with the way things were going in my life either. She had the house to herself, but instead of getting some action like I wanted, I received a cold hard slap to the face.

"Damn, Shantae, what the hell was that for?" I questioned.

"For leaving me alone for three months. The shit you're getting yourself into could have been avoided. What's wrong with you? Are you trying to throw your life away over some damn drugs?" she argued.

"Look, I'm a money man. I do whatever it takes, through any means necessary to get and keep money. I like the finer things in life, and that's how I'm going to go about it."

"So, money is all you care about?"

"Yup!"

"You don't care about me?" she whined at me sadly.

"Oh my God, you know I care about you, Shantae. Why'd you even ask me that? But I got to be honest. I love money, and I'm going to get it any way that I know I can," I answered, heading downstairs to the kitchen in an attempt to find something to eat. But the words that came out of my girlfriend's mouth hit me like a ton of bricks.

"You know it's more to life than just money, Karlos. You need to think about your future, our future."

"Girl, I'll be alright. Now, let's go get something to eat."

"Dammit, Karlos, I'm pregnant!"

"What?" I quickly turned right back around.

"What? Are you serious? How? I mean, oh my God! I can't believe this!"

"That's why I need you here. I don't want to do this by myself."

She cried with silent tears running down her cheeks. I wiped them away, kissed her forehead and embraced her with a hug.

"You don't have to worry. I'll never make you raise a child by yourself. I'll always be there for us. I love you, alright?" I reassured her.

I couldn't believe that I was going to have a daughter or son enter this world soon. Damn, I was scared as hell. I didn't know shit about being no father. Hell, I didn't even know where mine was. But what I did know was, I had to get my shit together. I had to be there for Shantae and the baby.

Hell, now more than ever, I needed money and I needed it fast.

I couldn't quite give up the drug life yet. I needed just enough to build a foundation then I'd quit, or so I thought...

CHAPTER 8

A RUDE AWAKENING

The words "I'm pregnant," scared me into the reality that I needed much more money and things in life that I could give Shantae. I had a decision to make. I could either try to live legit and hope that I get hired, but come now... What are the chances of people hiring a teenager with a spot on his record? Not likely, but even if they did, it still wouldn't pay me enough to provide for a family, so I had to man up and do what I had to do.

A meeting at a Quincy's house put everything in perspective for me.

"You know I respect you for taking the rap for the trafficking situation, very commendable."

"Yeah man, it was nothing. I just got ninety days."

"Ninety days? I know some dudes in this game who have done years behind this. That was a slap on the wrist if anything," he said, obviously putting off what I said.

"Anyway, I got a way you could make about $5k," he stated excitedly.

"Word! That's a lot of money, man."
"Yeah, I just need you to do a job for me. I need you to go to this address and retrieve a few items. You know, some supplies. He handed me a small

piece of paper with an address on it. On the other side of it was a list of supplies I was supposed to get him from his distributor.

I asked Quincy if Allen could come along with me on this trip to Chicago. But Q denied that real quick.

"No, this is a one-man job. Police will be on your head quick if they see a lot of dudes together in one car. Just do the trip. Go to that address. You going to talk to a dude name 'Paco.' You tell him you work for 'Q dawg,' show him my list. He gives you the supplies, bam! You come back here and supply it to me. We chop it, get it ready for sell. Make that money. Don't act scared, bruh!" Q joked to me with a mischievous grin on his face.

"What? You don't trust me or something?" he questioned.

I wanted to yell out, hell naw! But he was the biggest drug boss on Detroit's West side. What was I supposed to do?

"Besides, I don't trust Allen like I trust you. See, I know you're a loyal dude. You not going to steal shit from me. So, start out tomorrow morning, man. I'm going to check on you and make sure you're safe. It's all good, man. Don't be so worried. You get back, it'll be $5k waiting for you. Cash money in your hand." Q said for a man of his stature he sure had a lot of balls about shit "just going okay."

I should have known better. I should have thought of this as a fucking set up. But the only damn thing that was on my mind was being rewarded that $5k.

Later that night, I decided to sleep over at my girl Shantae's crib. Once her parents found out about her being knocked up, they made her get a place of her own. So, she moved in with her older sister, Tracy. It was cool, because it gave me a place to escape to beside my house.

Shantae was lying in bed watching a TV show on cable while I walked in looking tired and beat. She perked up once she saw me. I gave her a kiss on the lips and on the forehead. I couldn't help but touch her stomach. Eager to meet my little person someday soon.

"How was your day, Karlos? Why are you looking so tired?" she questioned.

"How come I don't see you at school anymore?"

"Cuz school isn't for me right now. I got to get money right now. But I want to hang in there and finish though," I reassured her.

"You still hustling, Karlos? I told you once the baby got here, I needed you to stop that shit!" she demanded.

"Look it isn't that easy to walk away from. If you were stripping at a club making $6k a night in tips, could you just suddenly stop dancing? Be honest, you wouldn't. Cuz you love that money. That green dollar sign. I got to get those Benjamins for real," I tried to explain to my girl.

"I won't need to strip. I just got accepted to Wayne State University as a pre-med major. My sister promised to help me with the baby if I stayed in school and keep my grades up to a B average. I'm excited. I'm going to be a doctor!" she exclaimed.

I couldn't be happier for my girl. She was so smart; she really was. Her only mistake was hooking up with a dude like me. She had so much to offer. I didn't even know what the hell she saw in me.

"Wow, baby, that's good. Congratulations. I'm about to lie down and get some sleep. I got a big day tomorrow."

"What do you have to do tomorrow?" she questioned me annoyingly.

"If you must know, I got to drive to Chicago to pick up a few things for my partner. You know, some supplies," I stated, not wanting to go into too much detail about anything.

"Mhmm, well, you just better make sure you stay your ass out of trouble. I can't afford to lose you." She giggled while rubbing her belly. I smiled back and held her in my arms until we both fell asleep.

The next morning, I got myself ready for this trip. For some reason, my stomach just felt weird.

Nothing I did could stop my stomach from rumbling. I should have seen this as a sign. My nerves were just getting the best of me. "Man up," I told myself. It was just my body's way of trying to talk me out of it. Then I remembered how bad I needed that $5k.

After, I got myself ready, I secured the note in my left jean pocket and my cell phone in the right. Shantae was still sleeping, thankfully. She only would have tried to continuously talk me out of it.

I made my way to my car and started out on my journey. While driving, I tried to steer clear of any cops, especially while driving on the freeway.

Last thing I needed was to get arrested. Quincy wouldn't want to hear that. Nope, it was a long drive, but I eventually made it to the Windy

City, better known as Chicago or as Hollywood Director Spike Lee put it, "Chi-raq."

I hate being in areas I never been in. I trusted no one to give me directions. I couldn't trust someone to help me. Anyone could be an undercover cop, I thought. After my stint in prison, I am a bit more cautious now. I stopped at the red light long enough to read the address on the note Quincy gave me. "1217 Athens Way, the old Warehouse."

It took me over an hour to find this place, and by now it was around 12 p.m. I received a few calls from family, but I just ignored them. It was time to handle business. I could answer them later.

I parked my car a block away from the building in case police or somebody was watching. I walked up towards this old abandoned warehouse with graffiti tatted all over. Apparently, gang affiliations had tatted it up in graffiti to stake their claim. No one had used this place in years, but I went in anyway. Once inside, I was greeted by a big burley clean-cut Mexican dude in an all-black suit.

"May I help you?" he questioned with authority.

"Um…I'm here to see Paco. I got a request to see him about supplies."

"Come right this way." He led me to the room down the hall where I saw people cutting, cooking and packaging coke, marijuana, ecstasy and other forms of drugs. The tough guy who offered me no name when asked led me in the back of the room where Paco and a few of his friends were.

Of course, Paco was another big burly, clean-cut Mexican guy. Paco was a scary looking guy. He had a few tattoos on his face and a big cut underneath his right eye. I could tell he was one person not to be messed with. He looked up at me with a harsh look on his face, studying me to see if I would pose any threat to him or his people.

"Well, what do you want? I never see you before."

Scared shitless, I stuttered through my words, hoping that I wouldn't die at this very moment.

"I was sent from Q dawg. I'm here to pick up supplies for him," I stuttered. I handed him the note with the instructions of what to get. All he could do was stare back at me, frowning, signaling for his men to gang up on me. I was ready to piss myself. What the hell have I gotten myself into?

"You say Q-dawg? I don't know no damn Q-dawg. Ah man this fool trying to run one over on us," he shouted out.

"He's from Detroit. He told me…I'm sorry. I'm just following orders," I cried out as one of his guards placed a semi-automatic gun to my forehead.

I immediately placed my hands up in defense. But what Paco did certainly surprise me. He began to burst out into laughter. The guard even removed the gun from my head. I just stood there confused.

"I'm just fucking with you. I know who Q-dawg is. I just wanted to make sure you weren't trying to start no shit with me. But yeah, I've been waiting on him to pick up his shipment. He got that good shit, too. Nothing but the purest Columbian coke," he stated. I felt a sense of relief. I grabbed the package and checked it out to be sure it was everything on Q's list and bounced out of there. That was the scariest forty-five minutes of my life. I cleared out of their fast. I concealed the supplies in my jeans. I wore baggy pants with a lot of pockets today for this very reason. I kept looking around my surroundings. I finally reached my car and attempted to exit out of Chi-town undetected. The moment I saw a police car coming down the street, I turned down another to avoid being pulled over. I did the speed limit and didn't bring attention to myself. Although, I was nervous as fuck. I tried to keep my cool to avoid looking as if I was up to something. Before I knew it, I was on the freeway headed back to Motown. I let out a sigh of relief. I successfully got through this trip without being pulled over. Riding on Woodward, all I could think about was getting that $5k and giving my new family everything I didn't have growing up. Shantae deserved that and more.

Around roughly, thirty minutes later, I pulled up to the house on Fenkell and Wyoming. I walked towards the back to see if Q was there. I walked into his room, but I must have thrown him off or startled him because this was the first time he snapped at me. Usually, we can always keep things cool. I wasn't sure why but for some reason he wasn't acting like himself. Something was up. I just wish I knew what it was.

"Hey Q man, I got that package you wanted me to get." I placed it on the table in front of him showing Q the measurements and weights of the drugs we were slinging on the streets.

"Damn, what took you so long? And didn't I tell you to knock before you enter my room. Shit, I could be doing anything. Don't just be barging in here like that. Didn't you learn that at home?" he rattled off.

"Damn, man. I'm sorry. I just wanted to show you that I got the pack—"

"I see. I see. Good job. I knew you'd do good. But I'm about to get out of here. I got to go out of town for a while. Got some sick family that I need to see," he tried to explain to me.

"Oh, for real, sorry to hear that? But what about that $5k you promised me? Am I still getting that?" I questioned.

"Oh, oh, um, yeah, the money. I almost forgot."

He reached inside of a small brown drawer and pulled out a white envelope and handed it to me. I looked inside and saw fifty crispy hundred-dollar bills all staring back at me. I shoved the envelope in my pockets and proceeded to walk out the door until…

"Where are you going?" Q questioned me suddenly.

"Um home, it's almost seven p.m. I've been driving all day. Plus, I'm tired. I want to get back to my family, man."

"You ain't got time for that. You got to help cut and package this stuff. We trying to hit downtown and Warren. Money don't stop just because you do."

"Man, can't I come by and do this tomorrow or next week…"

"What the fuck did I just say? Now sit yo' ass down and do what I tell you before I pop one in you," he threatened me while aiming a pistol at my head.

I had no choice but to follow his orders. I just wanted to go home. I was fucking tired. This shit was beginning to feel like slavery sometimes, *damn*!

"I'm going out of town, and I need to make sure my business still making money while I'm gone," he stated while grabbing his bags and heading towards the door.

"Well, when are you coming back?"

"Um, I don't know right now. Things are kind of sketchy with the family, but I'm sure y'all can hold it down from here," he replied as he turned to leave.

I thought it was funny how all sudden he had to go out of town and didn't know when he'd be returning. What good businessman leaves his business unattended like that? I joined the guys in the "shop" room--what we call our lab. We cut, cooked, weighed and packaged all the supplies before we sent them out to the streets to be bought. It was damn near 8 p.m., and I was tired and ready to go home. But something told me that wasn't going to happen tonight.

CHAPTER 9

QUINCY'S BETRAYAL (QUINCY'S POV)

I was about to become a free man. I walked out of that place with my bags packed ready to start a new life with my old lady somewhere in Jamaica and leave this drug shit alone. I made enough money over the years to retire somewhere special. I made the money while the little dudes did all the dirty work. I loved recruiting the naïve dudes off the street. Fill their heads up with how quickly they can get cash.

Then before I know it, they are the ones hooked like a drug while I'm about to make the biggest escape in my life.

While I'm walking outside, I see an all-black truck siting across the street. A person sticks their head out and motions for me to come see what they want. I knew this tactic all too well. I approach the vehicle, the guy inside, tells me to "get in."

I close the door behind me as I get in and see that it's a narc.

"So, where you headed to Q? Looks like you you're going somewhere."

"I'm getting the hell out of dodge is what I'm doing, man! Why you are acting like you don't know me, Steve?" I chuckled, giving my boy some dap.

"You know, the police sweating me hard out here. I'm trying to get out the game before I get taken out, ya feel me?"

"Yeah, I got you. How much you got on the Mary J?" Steve asked.

He always wanted me to hook up with something. But while I looked out for him. Steve always looked out for me and kept my ass out of trouble with the Feds.

Being a crooked cop could cost him his job, but it sure as hell protected mine, and in this world the only one I cared about was Quincy.

"But man, we got a quota, man. We trying to crack down on these drug rings. I have to give them something," he pleaded with me while rolling up a blunt to smoke.

"You know, I don't like to start shit, but if you take that house right there, it's about five or six guys in there with kilos of coke, weed, X, you name it. You could bust their asses right now." Yeah, I ratted out my squad, but I didn't give a damn. I wanted to live comfortable without living in fear of when I was going to get shot, arrested or even killed by some cop or drug dealer in competition with me.

"Oh alright, thanks. That's all the information we needed. I'll inform the DEA right now. You, my friend, have a safe trip to the airport, my brother."

I exited the vehicle and walked away a free man. I got inside my car without a thought of what could happen next. I was on my way to pick up my lady and we were off to Jamaica, baby, to live a better life.

A new life. To start over. I was forty years old and started in the drug game at sixteen years old. I was an old man but a wise man. I had friends all around. Enough to keep my ass out of federal prison. So, it was time to leave this life in the past and look toward my future.

CHAPTER 10

KARLOS'S UNEXPECTED SURPRISE

"Get your hands on the floor. Everybody get down. I repeat, everybody gets their asses down on the fucking floor. Don't look at me. Do what I tell you. You're under arrest for illegal drug possession, drug dealing and conspiracy. Hey, shut up! We don't want you to say shit, asshole!" The police came in yelling at everyone. I had nightmares about this happening. I just never thought it'd come true. Fuck, we'd been busted. They were raiding us and tearing the place apart.

"Get up, hey clear the house!" I heard one of the officers tell the others. Minute by minute, the DEA and other officers rushed our stash and confiscated not only our drug supply but our money. It was over.

One by one, officers placed us in hand cuffs and led us outside back to jail. I couldn't believe this.

Several people gathered outside to see what all the commotion was about. Officers tried to keep them away as much as they could. But the most embarrassing thing was when I saw Shantae running over towards me.

"Nooo! What's going on here? Why are you arresting him? Karlos no! Why would you do this? You told me—"

"Ma'am, I'm going to need you to back away. Excuse me, miss, I'm not going to tell you again. Back away from this area and go back across the street before we arrest you, too," the officer warned. I was devastated that I'd let Shantae down again.

The next couple days were the longest days I'd ever experienced. I was placed in a holding cell, until I was appointed a lawyer and was served a court date.

Today would be the day my life changed. I entered the downtown Detroit courthouse on Lafayette. This was the first time I'd been in front of an actual judge with jurors and a lawyer.

"We are here to discuss the case of Karlos G. Hunter vs. the city of Detroit. Mr. Hunter, you are on trial for drug conspiracy, dealing and possession. You were in trouble for this once before. Do you know the extent of your actions, son?" Judge Omar questioned.

"Yes, your honor, I do," I replied sadly.

"You are too young to be in here. You haven't even reached your eighteenth birthday. But sadly, you are going to have to spend it in federal prison. For the dealing of drugs and possession of drugs, you can serve up to ten years to life in prison. But, because you do have a rather decent record we hereby sentence you to five years without parole in Central Michigan Correctional Facility. You will be transferred there in two days. I hereby declare this case closed."

The judge just killed my life. I couldn't believe she sentenced me to five years in prison. Now, I see why Quincy left so quickly. He knew we were about to get busted. Had he stayed with us another day or two, Q would have received life in prison. But instead, I'm again taking the rap for this man's bullshit. Me, along with five other guys. One day, one of us had to find Q and smoke him out.

I saw my girl breaking into tears. My mother and brother were so hurt, they couldn't even look at me. The guard walked over to me to lead me back to prison. I had five years. Five long, hard years. The only thing I could think of was…damn!

CHAPTER 11

A MOTHER'S SORROW- (KARLTON'S POV)

My mother entered my bedroom with a heavy heart and silent tears running down the sides of her cheeks. She stood looking outside the window.

"I can't believe he's gone. He's out there somewhere, and I can't protect him from the world. They may try to harm him, and I can't protect him anymore, Karl. He's all alone," She wiped her tears with her hand.

I could feel the pain in my mother's voice.

"What did I do wrong? I tried my best to provide him with all I could. Why wasn't it enough? I don't see how you two turned out so differently." She turned to sit on the edge of my bed. The pain in her eyes showed every emotion that she wasn't courageous enough to muster up on her own.

"Promise me, Karl, when you go off to Michigan State today that you'll strive to do better. Make use of your education. Please do something meaningful. Don't waste your freedom," my mother advised me.

"You'll never have to worry about that. I promise to do everything in my power to make you proud." She smiled and gave me a tight squeeze.

"Oh, I'm sure you will. I'm sure you will."

I heard the loud horn of a car outside. I kissed my mom on the forehead, grabbed my bags and proceeded on out the door. It was time for me to depart from Detroit and head on to Lansing. This was the perfect time for me to start my political career. I was to become a city councilman to help troubled youth such as my nuisance of a brother Karlos. The sad part is he should have been going off to college right along with me but instead he's off in somebody's prison.

CHAPTER 12

SHANTAE'S PAIN (SHANTAE'S POV)

The pain of losing my boyfriend to something as foolish as drugs was completely unbearable. We were to go to prom together, but instead I ended up walking across stage without him. I gave birth to a beautiful little girl name Mariah Hunter. Knowing that he'd never have the chance to witness her as a baby is what truly broke my heart.

Well today, was a special day. I was driving to visit Karlos in prison. It would surely be a surprise for him. We've been writing each other for months. But it just wasn't the same.

When I made it to the visitor's gate I informed the guard I was there to see an inmate. He gave me a badge and walked down this long hallway. As I waited for his arrival, all I could think of is how barbaric it was ending up in a place like this. My heart sunk to my stomach once I saw Karlos's face. The stress of being confined to such a place took a heavy toll on him.

"Oh my God, Shantae. You have no idea how much this means to me." he said.

I hated talking to him through those damn prison phones and thick ass glass while guards monitored our conversations.

"Yeah, I know. I have someone I'd like you to meet. Your beautiful daughter Mariah."

I held her in my arms and saw the joy in his face as tears began to fall. He dropped the phone and cried harder.

"I'm so sorry. She's so beautiful. Wow, that's my daughter!"

"She's your-our daughter. Can you say hi to your daddy?" I laughed while trying to hold back tears my own damn self.

"Oh, I'm so sorry, Shantae. I never meant for things to get this bad. I just wanted to provide for you. I never thought it'd get to this point. It was never my intention to leave you out here struggling as a single mother. I can't wait to get the hell out of here. I swear, once I do, I'm going to live legit. I'm going to make money the right way and I promise you we will get married and have a real family. What have you been doing lately?" he questioned me.

"I've been coping, raising Mariah, plus I'm in school at Wayne State as a Pre-Med major. Studying to be a doctor is hard work!"

"That's awesome. I'm proud of you." He extended his gratitude, but I could see the pain and guilt of not being able to do more because his own life shattered his self-confidence. He learned from his mistakes. Unfortunately, it was just a little too late. He still had about four and a half more years left to serve.

The guard came and told us our time was up. He had to go back to his cell. I tried to hold back my emotions, but those tears burst through like a dam. Seeing Karlos so sad made me want to fight for him, but I couldn't. There was nothing I could do. He had to win this battle on his own. I placed

Mariah back inside the carrier and headed to my car. I cried all the way back home.

CHAPTER 13

KARLTON'S VICTORY (KARLTON'S POV)

ive Years Later

"I stand here before you a man of great integrity. I plan to help shape the city of Detroit into a town that is productive and fruitful. My colleagues and I will bring several jobs to the city. We will build schools, daycare and recreational centers. We will pass laws and get rid of old ones that no longer serve the city. I stand here as your councilman for the city of Detroit to do everything I promised in my campaign and more. Thank you very much!" I was so excited to be giving my first speech as city councilman.

My life was pretty good. I had the dream job. I even met and married my wife Sheila Houston, a MSU (Michigan State University) grad. We had two small children. We were to attend Harvard in the future. She and I would get our MBA in Law together. Sheila and I were to become the next Barack and Michelle Obama.

As I walked over to the table with the rest of the city council team, my assistant Rachel,

ran over to me with my cell phone.

"Sorry, Mr. Hunter, you have an important call. Your mother has been calling all day. She says it's urgent."

"Very well, thank you Rachel. I'll answer it." I retrieved my cell phone from Rachel and stepped inside the hallway of the Coleman A. Young Municipal building to see what was so darn important.

"Yes mother, I was just having a press conference."

"Oh, I know, but did you forget your brother gets out today

"Has it been five years already? Can't someone else pick him up? I'm obviously busy."

"No, plus you promised you'd do it remember?"

"Well promises are meant to be broken sometimes," I snapped off. I really didn't have time to do any of this. Nor did I want to. It wasn't my fault he got himself into trouble.

"No, you need to do it as soon as you are done. I don't want him wandering around and getting into even more trouble."

"Well, guess it's my job to babysit him," I said sarcastically.

"Can you please be nice to your brother? He's had a hard life you know. Can you try to help him get on his feet? He's still family."

"It's not my job to take care of him. He had the same damn opportunities that I was given, and now I'm supposed to feel sorry for him because he decided to blow his? Despicable!"

"Karlos! He is family. Just because you're successful now don't mean you can't go out and help your brother. Don't ever forget where you came from, Karl. You never know if you'll ever end up needing Karlos," my mother tried to preach to me, but I just wasn't going for it.

"Alright, to make you happy. Fine, fine. I'll go pick up my brother."

I finally ended my conversation with my mother. I found Sheila walking down the hall typing on her tablet. She was always busy. That's what I admired most about her. She remained focus and career-driven. I tapped her on the shoulder to grab her attention. Sheila smiled then looked up at me.

"We got to drive out to Central Prison right now."

"What? Why? That's all the way up north, Karl. What is the meaning of this?"

"My brother gets released from prison today, and I promised I'd be the one to take him home."

"Really, Karl. You're going to waste your gas on that inmate. Can't he have one of his jail or drug dealer 'homies,' come pick him up?" she questioned.

Sheila had no remorse for troubled youths because her ideality was like mine. You are responsible for your life. You're given the same opportunities as everyone else, and just because you choose to squander yours away, it's not society's responsibility to pay for your mistakes.

"Well, can you just try to be nice to my brother?" I begged.

"Sure, too bad we can't get him to reimburse us for gas." Sheila sucked her teeth, then grabbed the rest of her belongings.

The closer we reached the prison I could feel tension rising in my body. The nerves flowing through me felt like leaded pins. I was glad this was never a place I'd have to be. The 12-ft barb wire fence felt so much like entrapment. I just wanted to pick Karl up and get my ass right back to Detroit. I drove my pitch-black Mercedes towards the front entrance, and the person I saw walking towards me appeared as a replica of the brother I once knew.

His hair hadn't been kept up, but his tall, thin stature had become rather muscular. As much as I hated to admit it, I was happy to see him retain his freedom once more.

"Karlos!" I called out to him.

"Karl? Is that you? WOW! What have I missed within five years?" he joked in reference to my car and classy appearance.

"Why yes, it is? I also have a company car and lovely wife named Sheila." I pointed towards her to introduce them.

"Hello, Mrs. Sheila. I'm Karlos."

"I know who you are," Sheila replied in a snobbish tone.

"A company car? Wow, where do you work?" he asked getting inside the car, as we drove back home to Detroit.

"I just got elected city councilman of Detroit city. I'm into- "

"Politics! I can't believe it. My brother running the streets of Detroit."

"Yes, brother the legitimate way. Unlike what you were doing that got you tossed in prison." I stated in a conceding tone.

"You know, we really need to get past this. I've paid my big debt to society."

"Not big enough," Sheila mumbled under her breath.

"Look, are you going to patronize me the entire trip?" he questioned in a frustrated tone.

We finally reached our city of Detroit…Motown, and I pulled up to our old house where we grew up, where our mother resided. I told Sheila to go ahead inside as I walked over to my twin brother.

I stopped Karlos as he was going up the walkway and placed my hands on his shoulder.

"Look man, don't go in that house with that same 'street' mentality you've always had. I know you've had some screw-ups, but just try to think about Mom for a minute."

"Excuse me! When the hell did you become my damn father? I don't answer to you or anybody else. I am grown ass man."

"Look, I understand that. I just don't want you to wind up in any more trouble. You know, you're still young. You need to make something of yourself. Take me for instance. I graduated Magna Cum Laude from Michigan State University, plus I'm a city politician. I have a wonderful family. I'm just saying, I made something useful of myself while on this earth. What are you going to do with yourself?

"First of all, just because you graduated with some good grades and got a great job doesn't give you the right to look down your nose at me. Yeah, I did some pretty bad things. I sold drugs, trafficked drugs. I admit that, but like I said, I paid my debt to society. When are you going to get past that? I got my GED while I was on the inside, and I plan to do something with my life, but I what I won't be doing is spending the rest of it trying to please stuck-up pretty boys like you. Cause trust me, the same way I ended up locked up in prison, oh brother, it could happen to you..."

He tried to plead his sorry tired case to me.

"No, that'd never happen to me; I'm much too smart for that," I shot back.

As my brother raced up the stairs, I could see how out of touch with reality he truly was. He just couldn't contemplate the realness of how difficult it'd be for him to land a job once there is a conviction or offense stain on his record.

I've seen this one too many times. The ex-con tries to find work, but once he realizes his pickings are simply next to none, he's out to committing crime again, sometimes even more heinous and strenuous crimes. My brother had destroyed his life and hadn't even realized it. I mean, come on, where was he going to go with just a GED education. McDonald's, Burger King? Yeah right. That's laughable.

CHAPTER 14

KARLOS COMES HOME

Since I'd been, out all I could think about was seeing the ladies in my life. I rushed over to see Shantae. Repeatedly, I knocked on the door until she opened it. This time, I had to make things right by her. I prayed she hadn't changed her decision about being with me. The moment she opened the door, I almost wanted to cry. She looked so beautiful.

"Oh my God, Karlos, I can't believe you're out. It's been so long," she cried

"I know. I missed you so much," I admitted and gave her the biggest hug in my life.

"You look great! Wow, how have you been?"

"I've been living. I graduated from Wayne State University as a Pre-Med major. So now, I'm in their medical school program."

"Wow, you've been doing great!"

"Yeah, I'm going to be a doctor."

"That's good news, Shantae, but I must ask, how come you didn't come visit more when I was away?" I questioned, sadly.

"Are you serious? How could I? That's so damn selfish of you to ask. I didn't become a drug dealer and get busted. I had to work. I had to go to school. I had to take care of your daughter by myself, might I add. You promised me that you'd never leave me, and then you did. I even told you to stop doing what you were doing, but did you listen? NO! You just kept right on slinging that damn dope, and I'm sorry, Karlos. I love you, but I wasn't about to put my life on hold for you or anyone."

"All I can say is I'm sorry. I thought I was doing what needed to be done to provide for a family. I had to make sure we were straight and had money," I pleaded.

"Bull! That's complete bull, and you know it. Most men go out and find something called a job! Just be honest, you were addicted. You loved the money more than your family."

"I'm sorry. I never had a dad growing up and it's—"

"Karlos, stop making excuses. I didn't have a father either. A big percentage of people in America don't have a father, but you cannot keep using that as an excuse for bad behavior. You fucked up. Just admit it."

"Damn, Shantae. Why are you being so cold? But you right, I messed up. I was wrong for leaving you for five years alone to raise a child. I promise from now on, I'll live legit. Nothing illegal. I even got my GED. It's not a rewarding four-year degree like yours, but it's a start. And I promise Shantae, if you stick with me, I'll never leave you alone again. I want my family back. I want my life back. I want to experience my freedom again. So, I ask you today, will you marry me? I don't have a ring or anything. But I swear I'll work on it. I want to give Mariah something I didn't have."

I knew what Shantae said was correct. I had fucked up, and sadly, I must hold myself accountable. I just wanted a chance to make things right, not only with her but within my own life as well. She said, she'd give it a try, and I couldn't be any happier. When I saw my daughter, a few tears ran down my face. This little girl had grown so quickly. No longer a baby but a beautiful, brown-skin girl with the most beautiful face I'd ever seen. I just broke down crying. The fact that I missed out on so many years of her life completely broke my heart. She had no idea who I was and didn't want to bond with me.

How could I have allowed this to happen? Now that I was out, I had five years of making up to do with my princess. I wanted her to know who I was. I wanted Mariah to feel loved and wanted. I knew I had to get my life together for that little girl.

At this point, I vowed to myself and to Shantae that I was going to stay out of trouble with the law, and I meant it.

CHAPTER 15

KARLTON'S AFFAIR

The thing I envied about my brother was his ability to enjoy himself. He was so much more spontaneous than me. I've always been the serious, straight and narrow type. I've worked my ass off to get where I am, but now, I had to admit, well, I was kind of growing bored with the everyday routine. I might have been about my business, but I was a man nonetheless, and Sheila wasn't as exciting or fun to be around after two years of marriage. I tried to get her attention but…

I walked into the kitchen where I spotted Sheila with her nose in a book again. I quietly walked up to her and planted affectionate kisses on her neck and forehead. I was sure she'd get the clue but, not tonight.

"What are you doing? You know I'm trying to study to pass my bar exam before I go to Harvard next year," she spat out angrily.

"Sorry, babe. I just thought since the kids were asleep that we'd, you know..."

"Oh my God. Is that all you think about, Karlton? Goodness, there is much more to life," she replied, shooing me away.

"I know, but come on Sheila, I'm your husband, plus it's been three months already."

"I don't care how long it's been. We need to work and stay focused to keep this family together. We have children now, Karl. Honestly, get it together." She rolled her eyes and continued to bury her nose in those damn law books.

This was pretty messed up. Another, long, cold, horny night. I wanted to scream. Don't get me wrong here, I loved Sheila. I even loved her competitive and determined spirit, but there comes a time when enough is fucking enough. Books and degrees don't hold you close at night. I had become fed up and tired of begging my own damn wife to give me attention. Hey ladies, you guys aren't the only ones who deserve attention. We need and want affection, too, you know! It pained me to have to do this, but I had to get my needs met, and if it weren't through Sheila, then hey, I had to do what I had to do.

The next week at work, I was buried in paperwork. It couldn't get any worse than this. The judge brought up a new law ordinance to read and go over. Frustrated and overwhelmed was basically how I described the day.

I received a knock at my door, and in walked the cutest little blonde-haired woman. I had received a new assistant, and I had to admit, Ms. Amanda McKnight was looking damn good.

"Oh, I'm sorry to bother you, sir, but I had to drop off these papers before my lunch break."

"Oh, no problem. Just put them on my desk. Amanda, where were you planning to go for lunch? I questioned, hoping I'd be invited.

"Oh, I was just going to go to Bert's."

"I love that place!" I added.

"Why don't you come along? You can attend to this stuff later. I'm sure it'll be here when you get back."

I closed my laptop and grabbed my phone. I was hungry anyway, so I figured hell, why not? I got to eat, right?

While at the restaurant, we had a really great conversation about stuff, and I mean, just stuff. Not books, degrees, law, politics, or corruption plaguing the city, but fluffy stuff like music, movies and the weather. I hadn't had a good hearty laugh in a long time.

After we finished lunch, I sadly told her I didn't want to depart from her company just yet. So, we decided to continue by checking in at the Downtown Marriott Hotel. Yeah, I couldn't believe what I was doing, but Amanda was such a breath of fresh air to me. This was what I needed right now, but I panicked when I saw the hotel registration forms. I remembered how easily politicians can be caught up in career-ending scandals. I certainly couldn't risk losing it all because of this affair, so I signed in with my brother's name instead of mine. Hey, I was looking to try and cover my own ass by any means necessary, and with my brother's track record with the law, they'd easily suspect him over me.

Once I received the keys from the hotel staff, I led Amanda to the room. Let's just say that my three-month drought quickly ended after three hours! But as good as Amanda made me feel sexually, I couldn't get my mind off my wife. The guilt was beginning to run through my head. But not enough to stop seeing Amanda during my lunch breaks. She opened doors to my soul I never knew existed. The things she did my wife never even would think of trying. I fell completely in lust with this woman once she performed a blow job on me. I'd certainly never received that before.

When I happened to catch the time on the clock, it read 6:45 p.m. I needed to start heading home to my wife and kids.

"But I don't want you to go," Amanda whimpered.

"We're having too much fun," she said while rubbing my arm gently.

"Yes, I know, but I must get home to my wife and kids. They're waiting for me. I'm so sorry. I had a really great time tonight though," I reassured her.

"Will we ever hang out again, you know not just at the office?"

"Sure. We can see each other next week. Same hotel, same room. Bring something sexy this time," I joked with her.

I gathered myself in the bathroom. My reflection pained me. I couldn't believe what I had just done to Sheila. What kind of person had I become? I quickly showered and drove Amanda home. I promised to see her next week at the same time. This was a tricky situation I was getting myself into, but what was the harm in getting a little tail on the side? Every man does it.

The ride home was an unsettling one. I prayed Sheila wouldn't suspect anything. So, I came up with a lie that I planned to tell her to convince her I'd committed no wrongdoings.

I walked into the house and Sheila immediately looked irritated.

"Karlton, where have you been? The kids have been asking about you. I've tried calling and texting you, but you never answered your phone. What's going on? Is everything all right?"

"Yeah, honey. I just had to attend a last-minute meeting that ran kind of long. The judge brought in all these new laws and city ordinances we had to learn and go over. It was long and boring. I'm beat. I'm going to head to bed now," I obviously lied to my wife. I kissed her on the cheek and gave her the tightest hug I'd ever given, and we both headed to bed to sleep. I knew what I did was wrong, and I needed to stop with Amanda. But it felt so good. Nothing serious, right? Just some meaningless sex. I loved my wife, and I wanted to be with her forever, but a man had needs. And right now, Amanda fulfilled those needs.

CHAPTER 16

NOW, YOU'VE GONE TOO FAR!

Six Months Later

Amanda helped me to realize what I missed at home. She became sheer excitement to me. I could let loose in ways I hadn't been able to before. But I couldn't help but think of the sins I'd committed in front of God. I didn't want to lie to my wife anymore. I had to break it off with Amanda. But, how could I? I climbed off Amanda on the bed after I hit my climax.

Immediately, I went to the shower to get dressed. This wasn't going to be easy.

"Come on, Karl, why are you getting dressed so fast today? Usually, we go a couple more rounds after that?" she said flirtatiously while patting the mattress.

"I um...gotta get home. And I think we should stop seeing each other. I mean, this was good while it lasted, but I really can't go on hurting my wife like this."

"What? Your wife? Hell, what about me?"

"What do you mean, what about you? You knew I had a wife before we started messing around. Why is this coming as such a shock to you?"

"You're an asshole, Karlton!"

"Look, I didn't mean to hurt you."

"Fuck off, as long as you got what you wanted. Well, you know what. I wasn't going to tell you this, but I'm pregnant. Yeah, that's right, I'm pregnant. And if you don't tell your wife about us, I will go public with our affair. I'm your assistant. I really don't think you want that to happen, now do you? I mean, the last thing an honest politician wants is to get caught up in a nasty scandal. This could not only end your marriage, but your political career as well. I can make that happen. Just one little call to the media. It could all be over for you," she threatened me.

"You wouldn't do that. Come on Amanda, you're not pregnant. You're just being overly dramatic here," I stated as I tried to diffuse the situation.

"Oh really? I wouldn't do it. Yes, the hell I would. Tell your damn wife you're leaving her for me."

"What? I'm not leaving my family for you! Look, we just had a little fun, that's all. Why are you getting so worked up over nothing Amanda? Calm down, please. No need to be so hasty." I tried to calm her down. I had no idea why she began to get so riled up. I mean, I understand the disappointment she must feel. But why try to put my family in the middle of this.

Apparently, Amanda played no games because as soon as I dressed after my shower, I saw her with my phone in her hand.

"What the hell are you doing?!" I yelled.

"What does it look like I'm doing? If you won't tell your wife about us, I will. You can't just play with my emotions and put me back on the damn shelf now that you're done using me, Karl. It doesn't work like that."

"Give me the phone!" I yelled again.

I could see her getting ready to place the call to my wife, and that's when I began to panic. To try and take back control of the situation, I knocked the phone out of Amanda's hand. There must have been a fit of anger growing inside of me because the next thing I knew, I had my hands wrapped around Amanda's neck and I wasn't letting go. I could feel her trying to fight back as she began to dig her sharp nails into my skin. But the anger I felt towards this, and pardon my language, but this bitch over-clouded my judgement. I worked to get everything, and I do mean every damn thing, I've got in my life. I'm not going to throw it away because some silly chick doesn't know when to let go.

However, once I saw her eyes roll towards the top of her head and she ceased fighting, I realized that I'd gone too far. I didn't mean to kill her. I was in complete shock. What the hell had I done? I just wanted to scare her. I guess, I let my frustration get the better of me. In a panic, I grabbed my belongings and headed home as soon as I could.

I parked my car in the driveway and attempted to pull myself together before I walked into the house. Sheila was playing with the kids and smiled at me.

"Hey baby, how's your day?" she questioned.

"Um...it was...good. Yeah, honey everything was, ok. Thank you," I answered nervously.

The next week as I was eating dinner with my wife, I got the biggest shock in my life. We were watching a report on the news that a white woman was found dead in a hotel room at the Marriott. I started choking on my food as I tried to stomach the information I had just heard.

"What's wrong? Are you ok?" Sheila asked.

"No, I'm fine. My food just went down the wrong way," I told her, but deep down I was scared as shit. I couldn't let this get out, no matter what. Not even if it meant taking someone down to cover my own ass.

CHAPTER 17

KARLOS CAN'T ESCAPE HIS PAST (KARLOS POV)

Since I'd been out of jail, I had gotten a job fixing cars. Hell, not much, but it was a legal and honest job that was keeping me out of trouble. And, I'd truly been enjoying my time with my family. Mariah was beginning to adjust to me. We were sitting on the couch watching Saturday morning cartoons.

Shantae just smiled at us and returned to the kitchen to finish preparing breakfast for us.

"So, what's the name of this cartoon?" I asked my daughter.

"This is 'Super Why,' Dad! Don't you know?"

I couldn't help but laugh hearing this beautiful little girl that I helped create call me Dad. It was truly the best feeling in the world. I played and ran around the house with her, and between Mariah and Shantae, I truly found my purpose in life.

"What are we going to do today?" Shantae questioned.

"Well, I thought we'd go to the park later since you don't have classes today at the college, you know," I answered back.

"Yes, can I go to the park and get on the swings, please?!" Mariah asked excitedly.

"Sure, we'll go later today!" I answered.

But the next thing I knew, I heard a loud pounding at the door. Knots began to grow in my stomach because I knew the only people who knocked that hard were the police, and I had been living legit for about six months now. What the hell could they want? Shantae got up to answer the door, and four police officers stormed into our living room.

"Karlos Hunter, you're under arrest for the murder of Amanda McKnight."

"What? Murder? Who the hell is Amanda McKnight? I don't know who the hell that is. I've been with my family every day. I'd never murder anyone," I cried out. I couldn't believe this; getting arrested for a crime I didn't commit.

"How could you do this, Karlos? I thought you were trying to be a family?" "Shantae, I swear I don't know what they're talking about?"

The cops shoved me to the ground to "restrain me," but I wasn't even resisting to anything. One had his knee in my back while he handcuffed me in front of my daughter. My heart broke when I saw tears roll down her cheeks.

"Mommy, what are they doing? Why are those men hurting Daddy like that?"

All Shantae could do was take Mariah into another room. I was led to a squad car on my way back to prison, a place I vowed to never go back to, but this time I had no fucking clue why I was in trouble. When I arrived at the precinct, they informed me that a young Caucasian woman named Amanda McKnight had been murdered at the Marriott hotel. After I continuously pled my fucking case about not knowing this chick, they still booked me. I was thrown in an interrogation room. They wanted me to confess. Unlike the last time, I would have no problem snitching on anyone if it meant clearing my name and getting my freedom. But I had no idea what was going on.

"So, you mean to tell me that you have no idea about the murder of this Amanda McKnight? Look at this picture!" The detective tried to break me, but I was too familiar with their strategies.

"No, I told you. I don't know that woman. Never seen her a day in my life."

"But there are hotel rooms under your name. If you don't know her, how come you're spending time with her in hotels?"

"I'm not. I have a fiancé. I'm not interested in spending time with no other women. I swear to God, that I don't know this lady."

"You're trying to tell me somebody probably just framed you. Come on, Karlos, you can do better than that. Not only do we have evidence linking you to the crime, we have history to go on. But since you're not going to cooperate with us and give us the information that we need, we have no other choice but to send you to jail where you will await a court date that will later determine your sentence and jail time."

"What the hell? I didn't even do this. I'm going to jail for murder, and I didn't even do this," I continued to cry out. One of the officers punched me in the stomach and told me to shut the hell up and go quietly. My whole life was about to be over, and I didn't even know why.

Before they threw me in the slammer, I was allowed at least one phone call. I immediately, phoned my brother. I knew if anyone could help me, it'd be him.

"Man, are you calling me from prison again? Damn man, what the hell did you do this time, rob a bank?" Karl asked frustrated.

"What? Hell no. Why would you even say that? No, they got me down here because they think I killed some white chick named Amanda McKnight. I swear to God, brother, I don't know what they are talking about. I don't even know this woman. Man, please could come down here and clear my name. I was framed. I just want to go home.

"Oh, wow, that's crazy, Karlos. You've got yourself into a pretty messed up situation there."

"Yeah, that's what I'm saying. I need you to help clear my name or help do something. I'm completely innocent this time, I promise," I pleaded with my brother to bail me out.

"No can do, bruh. I'm tired of always bailing you out. You're a grown man, and I can't keep bailing you out every time you get into trouble."

"What? But I'm innocent! Karl, come on man. Karl! Hello! Hello! Karl!" My brother hung up on me and left me hanging. I couldn't believe it. The guard signaled for me to come with him. Sadly, I knew where I was headed. A damn jail cell. A jail cell for some shit I knew nothing about.

CHAPTER 18

THE COURT DATE

Six weeks had finally arrived, and it was time for my court date. I'd hope the judge would realize that I had nothing to do with this murder and let me go. Apparently, this was just one huge misunderstanding. I continued to walk down the corridor as police officers led me to the courtroom to hear the judge's decision. My heart was beating a mile a minute. There was no way I could receive a life sentence for a damn life I didn't even take.

"We are here to discuss the case of Karlos G. Hunter vs. The State of Michigan on the counts of involuntary manslaughter. Mr. Hunter, you look to serve 20 years to life in prison. Is there anything you'd like to say in your defense?" Judge Abernathy asked me.

"Judge, I didn't kill that girl. I don't even know who this woman is. I was at home with my fiancé and child, I swear…"

"Now, Mr. Hunter," he says, removing his glasses while pinching the bridge of his nose.

"This isn't your first time inside my courtroom. You've had plenty of troubles with the law in the past, and you stand here trying to tell me you didn't do this?"

"Your Honor, we honestly don't have true evidence that Mr. Hunter committed this offense," my lawyer stated.

"Yes, but we do have history. We all knew that it was just a matter of time before Mr. Hunter would move on too much bigger crimes," the DA said.

"Has the jury finalized their decision? Well, what is your verdict?" Judge Abernathy questioned.

"We, the jury, find Mr. Hunter guilty of voluntary manslaughter of Amanda McKnight," a female juror said.

Was the damn legal justice system this fucked up it had niggas going to jail for shit they didn't even fucking do! I'm sorry, but this was complete bullshit. I was found guilty and going to jail for life for ending a life I never knew existed. I turned to look at my lawyer, shocked and disappointed.

"I told you, I didn't do this. I told you this!"

"I…know I'm going to do everything that I can to see you get victory. They're just going by circumstantial evidence. Don't worry Mr. Hunter, I'm going to see you get justice," my lawyer promised while two big muscular prison guards began making their way over to me.

"Hey, let me have a word with my brother before you take him away," Karlton said.

"Hey, Karl, man. I didn't do this man. I swear to Jesus himself. I don't know how I got caught up in the middle of this. This is a case of mistaken identity. I told you I wasn't going to let you down no more," I cried.

"You know, Karlos, this really breaks my heart to see you like this?"

"Look at you, in an orange jumpsuit standing in handcuffs. You know you really disappointed me. Mom can't even bring herself down here to see you like this."

"But I told you, Karl, I didn't do this. I'm an innocent man."

"How many times have I heard that line before? He said to me before walking away to join his family. All I could do was turn away in embarrassment. I could kiss my life goodbye. It would no longer be filled with memories of watching my little girl grow up and seeing my soon-to-be wife by my side. Oh no, I'd be confined to the four walls of a jail cell. Damn, how could my life get this screwed up!

CHAPTER 19

KARLTON'S CONSCIOUS (FIVE YEARS LATER)

I had to say that it's unfortunate what my brother is experiencing right now. But what could I do? I'm just thankful that I could walk away with my marriage and political career intact. I couldn't afford to lose either one. I've worked too damn hard in life to have things taken away from me. Now my brother, he always wanted things to come easy for him. Life doesn't work that way. He ended up in the situation he was in because of his ignorant ghetto mentality. What was I supposed to do, hold his hand through life? No, if you ask me, good riddance to bad rubbish.

The next week, I was surrounded by reporters all asking how I felt to have a brother that committed murder. I answered the questions the best I could without giving myself away. Later that evening, at work during our routine monthly meeting, I got a rather odd question thrown at me by one of the local citizens.

"So, Mr. Hunter, how do you feel to have a brother that has committed murder?"

"Um, my brother and I are two completely different people and our personal lifestyles are not up for trial here. Let's stick to the current issues that are plaguing this wonderful city of Detroit," I answered nervously.

"But again, Mr. Hunter, aren't you the least bit worried about how this makes you look as a city councilman?" an over-zealous reporter chimed in rudely.

"I am not my brother's keeper. We are not one and the same. We took two completely different paths in life. Besides, I'm a politician with a law degree from Michigan State. I have earned my position rightfully so. It is not in my best interests to discuss my brother's criminal past. We all have someone in our family whom we are not proud of, and he is not up for discussion now. Now, if you don't mind, I'd like to get home now," I stated, walking away from the podium and taking off my microphone. I was done discussing why my brother was doing time in federal prison. He got what he deserved, and that was that. Later that evening, while I was eating dinner with my family, the missus and I were watching the evening news and heard some interesting information.

"Hey, turn up the TV. I want to hear this," I said to Sheila.

"Investigators believe that they have found a suspect in the Marriott hotel murder that claimed one victim's life. Amanda McKnight was brutally strangled to death inside a Marriott hotel room just a five years ago. According, to reports from police, the suspect is Karlos Hunter. Hunter has a criminal past of drug trafficking and possession. He was just released from a five-year prison sentence for these very same crimes. Now, Hunter may be facing up to life in jail for involuntary manslaughter and second-degree murder. Hunter is also the brother of Detroit city councilman Karlton Hunter. This is what he had to say about the incident."

The reporter cut to a blurb of me talking about my brother. I turned the channel to something else, and Sheila and I were just staring at each other in disbelief.

"You know with all the trouble your brother has been in, this certainly takes the cake. God! I know they say you can't pick your family, but possibly this jail time will be good for him. I mean honestly, honey, your brother is beginning to give your campaign leadership a black eye just because you are related to him. He really needs to get his act together. Of all the things, I would never have thought that he'd murder someone!" Sheila exclaimed.

"You know, I don't know what got inside his head. He was a good kid. Somewhere along the way, he lost his way in life.

"People like that just disgust me. Just a common thug," my wife added as she took her empty plate to the kitchen.

I couldn't get my brother off my mind. I had to see him. I had some words to say to him.

The next week, I made my way down to Central Federal Prison to pay Karlos a visit. A guard led me down to the visitor's room and told me to wait for his arrival. This was my first time I'd ever been inside a prison. Thankfully, I knew because of our positions in life, I'd never end up in here. That was the beauty of having an identical twin. Wrong yes, but I had a damn legacy to protect.

I finally saw my brother approaching the table. He wasn't looking too happy, but who would be? I watched him sit down at the table in his orange jumpsuit and small afro. He hadn't shaved in weeks. I guess prison life will do that to you.

"Man, I can't believe I've been in here this long for a crime that I didn't even commit. I miss my daughter. She's almost seven years old now. I miss my lady, Shantae. I told her I'd never make her a single mother. I just can't believe this. My whole world is gone." My brother sounded so sad and pathetic. I almost cared about his pain.

"Well, that's how it gets, my brother! You know the thing about being identical twins? I can easily get away with murder and pin this shit on you. I mean, who are they honestly going to believe? An honorable, city councilman or the brother who has a history of criminal offenses?

You're never getting out of here. I told you for years to change your life around, but did you? You're just a failure. Now, you get to take the rap for my crime and no one will ever believe in you. Enjoy your life, bitch…rotting inside that dreaded jail cell!"

"What the fuck you trying to say? You did this shit?" he questioned me.

"You never were too smart, were you? Read in between the damn lines." I laughed at him.

"You got me in here? You know I'm innocent. You got me in jail for nothing. Oh, I'm going to kick your ass. You got me stripped away from society, away from my girlfriend and my daughter. I'm going to kill yo' ass. You a dead motherfucka, Karl! Oh, I'm going to, once I get out of here. I'm going to find you and kill your ass!"

My brother mouthed off. Not the best thing to say in a prison, threatening to kill someone. Not a good look for him.

"Excuse me guard, the prisoner is being belligerent. He's threatening to kill me. Can you send him back to his cell?" I motioned for the guard to grab my brother, and as he was taken back to his cell, I laughed to myself. He was kicking and screaming nonsense. He now knows that he was the one framed for this crime that he didn't commit. There wasn't a damn thing he could do about it. I walked out of that prison a big man. I had done what most murderers wished they could. I had gotten away with cold-blooded murder. There was no way I could get caught. I was a politician, and I had a good, loving family. Now, with the dead weight out of the way, I was free to live and enjoy my life as I pleased.

CHAPTER 20

KARLOS' REVENGE FIVE YEARS LATER

I was at a loss for words. They say blood is thicker than water. Then, if that's blood, you can give me five gallons of water and let me die slowly. That punk-ass nigga ruined my entire life. He knew what he did was wrong, but instead of admitting his wrongs like a man, he'd rather let me suffer for it. Oh, ok, I had something planned for him. I was going to be sure I got justice. Who's the bitch now nigga? I was going to demand to speak to lawyers, anybody. I refused to rest until he was behind bars. If my life had to suffer, why not his? This was all because he didn't want to lose his cushy job running the city of Detroit. No, my brother, your wife needs to know not only that you cheated but screwed around and killed some chick you had no business sleeping with. I couldn't stand cowardly-ass men like him. I never once cheated on my girl, but now I couldn't even see her. He ain't got the right to take that away from me. I'm not resting until I get payback.

I was finally able to speak to my lawyer. I had to get him to look at the evidence. I know that there had to be something linking him to this murder. I sat impatiently in the room as my lawyer came in and sat down in front of me.

"So, what do you have for me?" I questioned tapping my fingers on the table hoping for some good news. But the look on his face said it all.

"Come on, man. I told you I wasn't anywhere near that woman. Can't they look at the surveillance video. I mean we don't look that much alike. What about the ID he used to check into the hotel? I mean seriously, damn!"

"The numbers used to check in the hotel matched yours? Apparently, he must've used your social security numbers—"

"That bastard! Can't there be something else? I know there's got to be something linking him to the murder. Come on, what about…has anyone ever checked his records, his date books?

He had to have had a record book that should have all his appointments in it. I know he had to have something hiding from his wife. I'm asking you to do this for me and my family. Please check his offices, his computer, something. I can't take the fall for this."

"You know, Karlos, I know you're a good kid that had a little trouble, but for you, I'll talk to the DA to re-open the case. We'll see what we can do to bring your case to justice."

All I had was the promise of my attorney, but something told me that I'd be a free man real soon. I just didn't want to get my spirits up just to be disappointed. Had to be honest, all of this began to take a toll on me. Tears began to fall from my eyes as I did everything I could to keep my composure.

Two weeks later, Steven Morgan, my attorney marched into the downtown courthouse. He was determined to get the case reopened for me. Morgan worked for me and was somewhat like a father to me. He was the only person who believed in me, believed that I was an innocent man. My lawyer stormed through the doors of Prosecutor Dean Clark with the files from my case. Clark was searching for a law book within his office. Once, he heard Morgan coming into the room, he turned around.

"Hello, Steven. What can I do for you today?"

"I need you to reopen the Hunter murder case."

"Why would I do that? We have the right black man behind bars. I'm not wasting taxpayer money on a closed case."

"Well, how can you be so sure? What if Karlos Hunter was innocent? I mean, have you checked out his brother Karlton and his whereabouts?"

"Karl Hunter is a respected and trustworthy politician and city councilman. Why would he do such a thing? What are you talking about? You're wasting my time Steven."

"Oh, I get it. He bought you off. He paid you to stay quiet. You know that it's illegal to take bribes."

"Hey, nobody here took any damn bribes. Even if I did, you couldn't prove that I did. It'd just be your word against mine, and we aren't wasting any damn taxpayer money reopening this damn case. So just drop it, Morgan!!!" Prosecutor Dean Clark slammed his hands on the large brown oak table.

"As attorney of Karlos Hunter, it is my duty to see him get the justice he deserves. You know damn well, Karlos didn't kill Amanda McKnight. I don't see how you can sleep at night knowing you had a hand in putting an innocent man behind bars, while her true killer walks free."

"I sleep peacefully knowing there is one less black man terrorizing our great city. That's how I sleep, Morgan. Why the hell do you care if this negro rots inside a damn jail cell?"

"You call yourself a prosecutor knowing you're letting money talk for you. You owe the city of Detroit an apology. I promise to report this to Judge Abernathy to see you get arrested right along with Karlton," he threatened, as he grabbed the file and exited the room.

"All right! I may know something. I'll give you a warrant to search Hunter's office and books. Long as you say I took no bribes. Let's just keep that little part between the two of us."

"Yeah, sure," Steven said, annoyed. He grabbed the paper and exited the courthouse.

Following that week, Morgan headed down to the city council building with a couple of police officers with hopes of finally putting an end to the murder of Amanda McKnight, but what he found shocked not only Steven but Karlton, himself.

Karlton was going over the city's budget plan for the new year when he received a knock on the door. He went to open it and was in disbelief at what he saw.

"What's the meaning of this, officer?"

"Hello, I'm Attorney Steven Morgan, and I have a warrant to search your office along with your record books. We have reason to believe you are involved with the murder of Amanda McKnight."

"Oooh no, there must be some mistake here. That's my brother. You have the wrong guy."

"No, sir. We have reason to believe that you are behind this murder," one of the officers replied.

"Karl, what are they talking about? Why are they now saying you were involved with this murder? Your brother did this, not you," Sheila said, puzzled.

"Uh…um…I don't know."

"Sir, we're looking at your old record books and wonder why there are dates of you and Amanda in your book at this hotel?" Morgan asked.

"She was my assistant, we worked on a lot of things together," Karl answered nervously.

"Karl, why would you go to a hotel with your secretary to discuss work?" Karl's wife questioned.

He turns to look at her. Unable to answer, he just shakes his head. Officers do more searching and find the exact date and time of the day when Amanda was at the hotel and died.

"Sir, were you meeting with Ms. McKnight on these dates?" Steven Morgan questioned.

"Tell the truth, Karl. I'm sure my husband had nothing to do with this. Now, will you please leave? We have work to do."

"Yes, sir, please tell the truth to your lovely wife as well as the city of Detroit. We already have all the evidence we need to book you. Video surveillance, text messages and your date books. You might as well confess right now."

"Well, if you have all this evidence, Mr. Steven Morgan, where was it when my brother was on trial. You obviously didn't have any of this shit then."

"That's because your dirty, rotten ass paid everyone else, including Prosecutor Dean Clark.

So, not only are you going down for murder but for bribery as well. Admit it, you paid off Judge Abernathy and a few of the jury members, too. All so you can keep your ass covered while your innocent brother rots in prison for a crime he didn't commit," Morgan ratted off to my brother.

Karlton knew the pressure was beginning to weigh him down. He couldn't contain his lies anymore. The truth was finally about to come out.

"Okay, fuck. I'm sorry, Sheila. I'm so sorry, Sheila!" My bitch-ass brother began to break down and cry.

"What?! So, you obviously slept with this woman. No man takes a woman to a hotel simply to discuss 'work.' Plus, in an effort to cover up your adulterous ways, you murder another human being. I'm done. Ya'll better take him away before I end up in jail for killing him myself. I want a damn divorce. Just please take him away," Sheila requested.

"Karlton Hunter, you're under arrest for the death of Amanda McKnight as well as the concealment of a murder and bribery of political officials," A couple of police officers barged into the room shortly after my brother confessed to the killing.

"The press is going to have a field day with this," Steven chuckled as the officers placed handcuffs on my brother. Finally, I was going to receive the justice I truly deserved. Karlton was led to the police car and eventually taken to the precinct. He had to have a trail before a judge who would ultimately determine his fate of the rest of life. When my attorney told me that news, I broke down crying. I wanted my life back. I wanted my freedom. I wanted to see my fiancé and my baby girl. I was soon released from my cell to be a witness at my brother's trial. How ironic was that shit?

The next month, I sat in a large room not as a suspect but as a witness. I felt vindicated seeing my twin brother standing in front of a judge in handcuffs. When the judge gave him forty years for the murder and some other counts thrown at him, I was conflicted with emotion. I didn't want my brother's life stripped away, but at the same time, he had to pay for his past transgressions. Before he was taken away to a prison cell, I had to take one last look at my brother. Had to speak my peace to him.

"Damn brother, look at you. You've become everything you, yourself despised. I can't believe you did this to me. You always thought that you were so much better than me. But see how the tables have turned. You're going to the very place I've spent most of my life, away from your kids and your wife. All I wanted was respect from you. Then you go and blame me for a murder I didn't commit. You deserve everything you get. I love you man. But this was wrong. Now, you going to know how it feels to have your life stripped away from you. Karma's a bitch, ain't it, my brother," I smirked at him as I walked away, and he couldn't do anything but hold his head down in shame.

"I'm so sorry, Karlos," he apologized sadly before he was taken off to prison. I walked out the city courthouse and was greeted by my daughter and fiancé waiting on me by the car. I cried tears of joy to be finally reunited with my family. I could now make up for lost time. Karlos Hunter, is home. I am finally home.

COMING DECEMEBER 1ST, 2018
SLEEPING WITH THE ENEMY

CHAPTER 1

MY STORY

I am posted by my locker waiting on this English class to start. I see Melissa Owens, the finest chick in the whole Chanson school. She walks past me every day. She is perfection everywhere from her titties, ass and hips, but she was a complete bitch. Melissa was the meanest and most stuck up girl I've ever met. All that beauty must of went to her head because she walks around like she the shit. I'd like to fuck the shit out of her then beat the shit out of her for messing with my little sister Geneva.

"Hey, Geneva, where did you get that shirt from? I really like it."

"Thanks," she says.

"Yeah, I liked it when it came out last season. Damn, why are you so poor? I feel so bad for you.

Hell, if it wasn't for your brother, I'd feel sorry for you," she said laughing as she walked away.

Melissa made her way over to me. I played it cool like I always did. I let the hoes come to me like they always do with their stupid asses.

"Hey Jeff, what's up? You look good today."

"What? Today? I look good every day. But why you always bagging on my sister. That shit ain't cool, Melissa."

"Okay, I'll stop. But I can't believe you two are related. You're so different."

"What' sup with you and me?" I asked as I pulled her by the waist closer to me and stared deep into her eyes.

"I don't know what is up with us. That's your call. What are you doing after school?"

"You, if you let me?" I said to her. I couldn't believe how fast girls eat this shit up. I mean damn! All I said was what she was doing after school, and the bitch was putty in my hands.

"What time you free?"

"I'm free whenever you are, Ms. Melissa. Just one thing I have to know; my place or yours?" I whispered into her ear.

"We can do it at my place. I don't live that far away from here."

"Alright, just hit me up after your last class."

"I sure will."

"Alright, sweetie, I look forward to it," I said as I gave her a little pat on the behind. She looked back at me and smiled as she walked away to class. My sister walked right up to me and punched me lightly in the chest.

"What, Geneva?"

"How can you mess around with her after the way she treats me?"

"Stop worrying. I put a stop to all that. You won't have to worry about her messing with you anymore after I'm done with her ass tonight."

"Jeffrey, please tell me you're not going to do what I think you are."

"What's that?" I laughed.

"You can't!"

"And pass up on that phat ass. I don't think so, little sis! But trust me; she won't be the same after being with me."

"You are a mess! You are talking about…you are going to…"

"Shh! everybody doesn't need to know. Aren't you late for class sweetheart?"

"You lucky. I'll see you at home."

"Alright, order something. You can't cook!"

"Shut up!"

I loved my sister, she was the only one that meant something to me. Nobody else mattered to me. I didn't give a fuck about nothing or no one. I was all about me and I didn't give a fuck. My pops already scarred me for life, so why should I care about the thoughts and feelings of others. I just hate selfish people who mess with mine.

I finally made my lazy ass go over to my English class, but Mr. Pratt was late, so I decided to catch up with a few of my boys who were in the class with me.

"Hey, Jeff man. I heard you were down with Melissa Owens. Man!! Do you know about her?"

"What, that she fine as fuck?"

"Naw man, she out there. She'll do it to just anybody I heard," Bryant, one of my friends said.

"Shit, probably true man. Look at the body on her. You can't tell me ole' girl ain't been around the block, but she ain't gone know what to do once she done with me."

"I feel you on that one, man," my friend Scott said.

My teacher finally made it in talking about how he was running late because he had a flat tire or some shit. I was half listening. I was thinking about nailing Melissa's fine red-bone ass. I couldn't wait to get her alone.

Later that day, I met Melissa at her locker talking to a couple of friends. I tapped her on the shoulder, and I guess she was startled because she looked surprised that I was standing in front of her.

"You ready?"

"Oh yeah, I am ready."

"You change your mind or something?"

"No, I just thought you were going to back out."

"No, I thought you were going to back out. Hello ma," I said to her friend Jennifer, a short little brown-skin cutie. She wanted to be like Melissa so bad. I could tell she wanted me, too. Maybe once I was done with her, I'll bone her friend later.

"Alright, I'll talk to you later Jennifer."

"Alright, call me later girl!"

Melissa just smiled and turned. She put her arm around my waist and kissed me on the cheek. This girl just didn't know what she was doing to me. I was ready to take her right now. We walked to Melissa's car and she drove us over to her place.

Melissa had a nice home in a quiet little suburban neighborhood. She was a spoiled kid who got whatever the hell she wanted. And right now, she wanted me, and I was about to let her have it.

"So where are your parents at?"

"At work of course, they don't come home until midnight."

"Mmhm, I like the sound of that. Look at y'all got plasma screens and entertainment systems. I'm gon have to challenge you on that Xbox!"

"Naw, I'm pretty good at that. I'll kill you in some Madden."

"Whatever. But we know this ain't what we came here for. So why are we stalling?"

"My bedroom is in there," she said pointing to a closed door.

"Come on."

She didn't waste any time heading to the room. We locked the door just in case. I lay out on the bed then she climbed right on top of me.

"Why you want to be with me? It's so many girls in our school."

Because you're easy, damn! Why do girls always kill shit by talking? Just let me nut and get the fuck on, shit! I got other things to see and other people to do. Yeah, I meant what I said.

"I like you. You know that. Melissa, you know you're the prettiest girl in that school. Why you even ask a question like that," I said as I started to gently caress her thighs and her ass. She leaned into me and began kissing me passionately. She rubbed her hand up and down my chest, and suddenly, her hand made its way to my dick. This girl was a true freak! I knew what everybody was saying about her was true. I couldn't believe how forward she was. The way she grabbed hold of me and told me how she wanted me to do her. I knew it would be on.

I thought about asking if this bitch had protection, but what the hell? If she doesn't say shit, I won't say shit either. I was ready to pound her ass, so I could go back to my boys and tell them how good it was to be with Melissa Owens. I flipped her over and started feeling in between her legs. Women love that shit, love getting that pussy wet. I took pleasure in hearing the moans come from her as she grabbed on to my shoulders. I began to undress her and was pleased at what I saw. My hands rubbed against her D-size breasts. I was going to lick this girl out. I finished undressing and was ready to lay the pipe down on this broad. I lay her down, looked deep into her eyes and entered her warm, moist pussy. This shit, never felt so good. What felt even better was listening to her moan my name repeatedly. Only, if she knew what she was about to get from me. Repeatedly, I penetrated her and enjoyed every minute of it, making her come numerous times. After I released my deathly venom in this trick, she motioned for me to take the subway. I happily obliged. This silly girl just didn't know what I was going to do to her.

Melissa screamed my name repeatedly as she grabbed hold onto me. The way she yelled and kicked as she squirmed all over the bed was the highlight of all of this. Creating a water fall in between Melissa's legs made me want to enter her again. Apparently, she was surprised that I would do just about everything with her, because I was tearing that ass up. I bust my fourth nut and called it a night. It was getting late anyway. I had been over there for like five, almost six, hours. She looked worn out anyway. I kissed her on the cheek and started to put back on my clothes.

"Are you alright, Melissa?"

"Yeah, I just wasn't expecting all of that!"

"Well, now you can tell all of your friends how good my dick is."

"Whatever!"

Because best believe, I'm going to tell them how good your pussy was.

"I'll call you, Mel. Don't have wet dreams about me!"

"Shut up! Alright, goodbye Jeff. I'll see you tomorrow."

I walked home from Melissa's house, which wasn't too much farther from where I stayed. I felt really good after fucking Melissa. I felt bad for her, but she probably deserved it. I hope my sister made something to eat because I was starving. We didn't stay with our parents; we are on our own. My father has life in prison for murdering our mother. Yeah, I got a pretty fucked up life. Lucky for Geneva, she has a different father from me. I was glad she was adopted and wasn't a bastard like me. She deserved better than the life that I had. I walked into the house and smelt the faint smell of spaghetti and garlic bread.

"Hey, Geneva, what's up?!"

"What the hell are you doing coming home so damn late? It's eleven thirty."

"I told you. I was with Melissa!"

"What, Jeffrey, don't you ever feel bad about what you do to these girls?"

"No! Why should I feel bad? She wanted to fuck me? Damn, I should've made her suck my dick!"

"J! Come on!"

"Why do you care so much about her? She treats you like shit?"

"But she still doesn't deserve to be given a death sentence."

"Look, what do you want me to do, 'Neva? There is nothing I can do. What do you want me to do, not have sex?!"

"Yes!"

"I didn't do this to myself, it happened to me. I'm not going to stop something I enjoy just because of some fucked up shit. I like sex. I love sex. So, leave me alone. I'm hungry. Where is the food at?"

"It's in the microwave. I'm going to bed."

"Goodnight!"

I knew my sister worried about me. But I was 17 years old, going on 18. I was all she had. I had to deal with some horrific shit because my father was out there. How the hell is that my fault? If I could, I'd go to that prison and beat the shit out his ass. I hope I don't end up in there with him one day. But right now, I enjoy pussy and the feeling I got from having sex and have no plans on stopping anytime soon.

The next day at school, I was standing outside the building waiting on homeroom to begin when Bryant and Scott approached me wondering how my one-night stand went with Melissa.

"I know you uh, put it down on her right?!" Scott asked.

"Man, what you think? She got exhausted after I bust for the fourth time," I said as they all began to burst out with laughter.

"Shh, there she is," I said as Melissa was making her way towards the door with a few of her friends.

"Hey, what's up Jeffrey?"

"What's up baby? How are you doing?!"

She continued in the building as we stood outside. Melissa and her friends walked over to the cafeteria to grab some breakfast before class started.

"So, girl, come on, tell me how it was! I know that Jeffrey is so good looking!" Jennifer said. She was more like a follower behind Melissa.

"Wait, did I miss something?" Nadia questioned.

"I had sex with Jeffrey last night!"

"What, are you serious?"

"Yes girl! Let me tell you! His penis is so big! He knows exactly what to do with it, too! I mean we did it over and over again. He went down on me too, girl! I mean we did just about everything last night. I am telling y'all he is good. I got to have him again."

Geneva happened to be walking past and heard Melissa talking about the rendezvous she had. She walked up to her trying to get her attention.

"Uh, Melissa, I need to tell you something."

"What the fuck would you need to tell me, loser?!" she says, as her friends begin to cackle with laughter.

"Look, I know you don't like me, but I seriously need to tell you something. It's about my brother."

"I already know everything there is to know about your fine ass brother. Girl, did I tell you that he lasted for almost six hours! I mean whoooooooooo! I was exhausted!"

"Melissa, I don't mean to be nosey, but did you happen to use a condom with my brother?"

"What? Why? I'm on the pill. He ain't gon get me pregnant? And damn, why the fuck is you still here all up in my business! Get away from me!"

"You know what?! You are a bitch Melissa, and you deserve what my brother just gave you!"

"What, bitch? Who the hell you calling a bitch? I'd kick your ass!"

"Hey, Melissa, calm down." Nadia tried to calm her down.

"I don't know what the hell her problem is!"

"Hey, I think I should be heading to the library now. I have to print out a paper before I go to class."

"Alright, goodbye Jennifer. See you later."

"But don't you think she might have been trying to tell you something about him. And why the hell didn't you use protection. I mean I know he is finer than no other, but don't you think that he probably sleeps around? A lot of girls like him, Melissa."

"So, that don't mean he sleeps with them. I got tested two months ago and I'm clean. Please stop worrying about me. Let's get ready for class."

Melissa and Nadia made their way out of the cafeteria, but Geneva still wanted to warn Melissa. She pulled her by the arm and whispered in her ear.

"My brother has…"

"What, what is it that you need to tell me about him so damn bad?"

"Look, all I can say is you might want to watch yourself around him. He isn't who you think he is."

"All I can say is you need to leave me alone. I am with him and I don't need you trying to persuade me to leave him. Leave me alone, damn!" she said, as she walked out of the cafeteria.

That was what I was talking about. Some people just didn't have any disregard for anything. Now later, when she finds out what's really going on, she'll blame her for not warning her. But by then, it'll be too late. In those six hours I spent pleasuring her sweet body, it took only six minutes to destroy her sweet little body.

Author Janae Marie, is an American writer, publisher and entrepreneur. Janae was born in Detroit, MI. and has earned a Bachelor's Degree in Media Arts & Studies from Wayne State University. She began writing novels at the age of 16 and published her first book at the age of 25 entitled, Flirting with Temptations. A follow-up novel was later published two years later, Daddy's Home. She is also the publisher of The Hot Scoop Ent. Magazine, an urban entertainment magazine that caters to minorities doing admirable things in and around their community. She now resides in California with her daughter.